PENGUIN BOOKS

FINDING YOUR ELEMENT

Sir Ken Robinson, PhD, is an internationally recognized leader in the development of creativity, innovation and human potential. He advises governments, corporations, education systems and some of the world's leading cultural organizations. His famous 2006 talk to the prestigious TED Conference is the most watched video on TED.com with over 15 million views to date.

Lou Aronica is the author of two novels and coauthor of several works of nonfiction, including *The Culture Code* (with Clotaire Rapaille) and *The Element*.

Finding Your Element

*How to Discover Your Talents and
Passions and Transform Your Life*

KEN ROBINSON, PHD
and Lou Aronica

PENGUIN BOOKS

PENGUIN BOOKS

Published by the Penguin Group
Penguin Books Ltd, 80 Strand, London WC2R 0RL, England
Penguin Group (USA) Inc., 375 Hudson Street, New York, New York 10014, USA
Penguin Group (Canada), 90 Eglinton Avenue East, Suite 700, Toronto, Ontario, Canada M4P 2Y3
(a division of Pearson Penguin Canada Inc.)
Penguin Ireland, 25 St Stephen's Green, Dublin 2, Ireland (a division of Penguin Books Ltd)
Penguin Group (Australia), 707 Collins Street, Melbourne, Victoria 3008, Australia
(a division of Pearson Australia Group Pty Ltd)
Penguin Books India Pvt Ltd, 11 Community Centre, Panchsheel Park, New Delhi – 110 017, India
Penguin Group (NZ), 67 Apollo Drive, Rosedale, Auckland 0632, New Zealand
(a division of Pearson New Zealand Ltd)
Penguin Books (South Africa) (Pty) Ltd, Block D, Rosebank Office Park,
181 Jan Smuts Avenue, Parktown North, Gauteng 2193, South Africa

Penguin Books Ltd, Registered Offices: 80 Strand, London WC2R 0RL, England

www.penguin.com

First published in the United States of America by Viking, an imprint
of Penguin Group (USA) Inc. 2013
First published in Great Britain by Allen Lane 2013
Published in Penguin Books 2014

014

Copyright © Ken Robinson, 2013

ISBN: 978-0-241-95202-3

www.greenpenguin.co.uk

Penguin Books is committed to a sustainable
future for our business, our readers and our planet.
This book is made from Forest Stewardship
Council™ certified paper.

*For Peter Brinson (1920–95), an inspiration and mentor
to me and to countless others on how to live a full and
creative life by helping others to do the same.*

Acknowledgments

This book was born out of the tremendous response to its predecessor, *The Element: How Finding Your Passion Changes Everything.* As always, there are too many people to thank individually, but some have to be mentioned or I'll never hear the end of it.

First and foremost, I have to thank Lou Aronica, my collaborator on the Element books, for his constant professionalism, expertise, and essential good humor from start to finish. We both owe special thanks to our literary agent, Peter Miller, for his (not always) gentle nudging to get the sequel under way in the first place and for his expert representation of it to publishers in so many countries once it was done. At Viking, our commissioning publisher in the United States, Kathryn Court and her associate editor Tara Singh have been wonderful creative partners in taking the book through all the stages from the first hopeful outline to final publication. And our assistant, Jodi Rose, has been a rock of reliability in helping me manage a tight writing deadline in a tangle of other commitments and travel.

At this stage, many writers include an apology to their family for having to put up with long months of silence and brooding preoccupation. I certainly owe that to mine. I also have to thank them for helping to make this book a family affair. I wanted this to be a book that families could read and share and I enlisted my own to make sure it was. In between writing and publishing her own book, *India's Summer*, my wife, Thérèse, offered a stream of thoughts and encouragement for this one as successive draft chapters rolled off the laptop. Our daughter, Kate, read every word of the manuscript and road tested all of the exercises and helped me design many of them. She was a tremendous source of encouragement and inspiration as we tested the tone and style of the book. Our son, James, has a special interest in, and deep knowledge of, spiritual questions and offered some expert comment on those sections of the book. He also drew the graphic of the Mind Map, embarrassing my own amateur attempts to do the same. My brother John Robinson, an accomplished researcher, helped with investigating numerous questions and checking many points of detail to make sure that what we say is not only valuable but also true. I'm deeply grateful to them all.

Last and of course not least, we have to thank the many people of all ages from around the world who read the first book and then contacted us with their own Element stories. We had far more than we could include in this new book but they all underline the heart of the argument that people in all walks of life really do achieve their best when they find their Element. Their responses and questions made it clear that there was a real value in a sequel, and that's what you now have in your hands. I trust we've done justice to them and to you.

Contents

Introduction

The aim of this book is to help you find your Element.

I was in Oklahoma a few years ago and heard an old story. Two young fish are swimming down a river and an older fish swims past them in the opposite direction. He says, "Good morning, boys. How's the water?" They smile at him and swim on. Further up the river, one of the young fish turns to the other and says, "What's water?" He takes his natural element so much for granted that he doesn't even know he's in it. Being in your own Element is like that. It's about doing something that feels so completely natural to you, that resonates so strongly with you, that you feel that this is who you really are.

What about you? Are you in your Element? Do you know what your Element is or how to find it? There are plenty of people who live their lives in their Element and feel they're doing exactly what they were born to do. There are very many who do not. Consequently, they don't really enjoy their lives; they endure them and wait for the weekend.

In 2009 we published *The Element: How Finding Your Passion Changes Everything.* That book is about the difference between these two ways of living and the difference it makes. The Element is where natural aptitude meets personal passion. To begin with, it means that you are doing something for which you have a natural feel. It could be playing the guitar, or basketball, or cooking, or teaching, or working with technology or with animals. People in their Element may be teachers, designers, homemakers, entertainers, medics, firefighters, artists, social workers, accountants, administrators, librarians, foresters, soldiers, you name it. They can be anything at all. I was talking recently to a woman in her early sixties who has spent her life as an accountant. As a child at school she understood numbers right away and became fascinated by mathematics. She just "got" it. So an essential step in finding your Element is to understand your own aptitudes and what they really are.

But being in your Element is more than doing things you are good at. Many people are good at things they don't really care for. To be in your Element you have to love it, too. That was true of the accountant. She wasn't just good with numbers. She relished them. For her, being an accountant was not work at all. It was what she loved to do. As Confucius said, "Choose a job you love, and you will never have to work a day in your life." Confucius had not read *The Element*, but it feels like he did.

The aim of *The Element* was to encourage people to think differently about themselves and the lives they could lead. It's had a wonderful response from people of all ages from all around the world and has been translated so far into twenty-three languages. At talks and book signings, people often tell me that they're buying *The Element* because they're looking for a new direction in their own lives. Others say they are buying it for their children, for their partners, for their friends or their parents. I always ask people what they do and if they enjoy it. No matter what they do, some say spontaneously, "I love it," and their faces light up. I know right away that they have found their Element. Others hesitate and say something like, "It's okay for now," or, "It pays the bills." I know they should keep looking.

Why is it important to find your Element? The most important reason is personal. Finding your Element is vital to understanding who you are and what you're capable of being and doing with your life. The second reason is social. Very many people lack purpose in their lives. The evidence of this is everywhere: in the sheer numbers of people who are not interested in the work they do; in the growing numbers of students who feel alienated by the education system; and in the rising use everywhere of antidepressants, alcohol and painkillers. Probably the harshest evidence is how many people commit suicide every year, especially young people.

Human resources are like natural resources: they're often buried beneath the surface and you have to make an effort to find them. On the whole, we do a poor job of that in our schools, businesses and communities. We pay a huge price for that failure. I'm not suggesting that helping everyone find their Element will solve all the social problems we face, but it would certainly help.

The third reason is economic. Being in your Element is not only about what you do for a living. Some people don't want to make money from being in their Element and others can't. It depends what it is. Finding your Element is fundamentally about enhancing the balance of your life as a whole. However, there are economic reasons for finding your Element.

These days it's probable that you will have various jobs and even occupations during your working life. Where you start out is not likely to be where you will end up. Knowing what your Element is will give you a much better sense of direction than simply bouncing from one job to the next. Whatever your age, it's the best way to find work that really fulfills you.

If you are in the middle of your working life, you may be ready for a radical change and be looking for a way of making a living that truly resonates with who you are.

If you're unemployed, there's no better time to look within and around yourself to find a new sense of direction. In times of economic downturn, this is more important than ever. If you know what your Element is, you're more likely to find ways to make a living at it. Meanwhile, it is vitally important, especially when money is tight, for organizations to have people doing what is truly meaningful to them. An organization with a staff that's fully engaged is far more likely to succeed than one with a large portion of its workforce detached, cynical and uninspired.

If you are retired, when else will you deliver on those promises to yourself? This is the perfect time to rediscover old enthusiasms and explore pathways that you may once have turned away from.

Although *The Element* was intended to be inspiring and encouraging, it was not meant to be a practical guide. Ever since it was published, though, people have asked me how they can find their own Element, or help other people to find theirs. They asked other questions too, for example:

- What if I have no special talents?
- What if I have no real passions?
- What if I love something I'm not good at?
- What if I'm good at something I don't love?
- What if I can't make a living from my Element?
- What if I have too many other responsibilities and things to do?
- What if I'm too young?

- What if I'm too old?
- Do we only have one Element?
- Is it the same throughout our lives, or does it change?
- How will I know when I've found it?
- What do I do to help my children find their Element?

There are answers to these questions, and as the success of that first book grows, I know that I need to offer them. *Finding Your Element* is a wholehearted attempt to do just that. So, whatever you do, wherever you are and no matter how old you are, if you're searching for your Element, this book is for you. You may be:

- frustrated that you do not know what your real talents and passions are
- at school, wondering which courses to take and why
- trying to decide whether to go to college or to do something else instead
- in a job you don't like and wondering where to turn
- in midlife or later and feeling the need for a new direction
- unemployed and trying to work out what to do now.

If you know people who are searching for their Element, this book is for them too.

What's in This Book?

Finding Your Element is the natural companion and sequel to *The Element*. It builds on the core ideas of *The Element* and offers advice, techniques and resources to put those ideas into practice in your own life. This new book has ten chapters. Chapter One sets out the basic principles and ground rules for finding your Element and why it's so important that you try. Chapter Two is about understanding your own aptitudes, and offers tools and techniques for doing that. Chapter Three looks at why you might not know the real depth of your natural abilities and what you can do about it. Chapter Four is about discovering your passions and what that really means in terms of finding your own Element and feeding your own spiritual energy. Chapter Five explores the idea of happiness and how finding your Element can increase it in your own life. Chapter Six focuses on your own attitudes and whether they're holding you back or moving you forward. Chapter Seven helps you to take stock of your current circumstances and create opportunities for change. Chapter Eight is about connecting with others who share your Element and how to do that. Chapter Nine helps you to draw together an action plan and to take the critical next steps. Chapter Ten is a reflection on the main themes of the book and a reinforcement of why you should take this journey in the first place.

There are five main thematic threads that weave throughout the whole book, each of which is intended to help you reflect and focus on finding your own Element.

Ideas and Principles

Each chapter sets out ideas and principles to clarify what being in your Element really means and how this may manifest in your own life. This book draws on the arguments of *The Element*. It also introduces many new ideas that are essential to finding your Element and to knowing when you've found it. They include ideas about aptitudes and ability, learning styles, passion, attitudes and personality, happiness and purpose.

Stories and Examples

The book includes many new stories from people in all walks of life about how they found their own Element, what it took to do that, and the difference it has made to them. Many of these stories have come from people who read the first book and were inspired to tell us about how these principles have played out in their own lives. The Element is different for each of them, as it is for everyone. Often it is very specific: not teaching in general, but kindergarten or adults; not all music, but jazz; not all sports, but basketball or swimming; not all science, but pathology; not writing in general, but fiction for women. The reason for telling these stories of other people's paths is to help you plan yours. Their purpose is to inspire you with real examples of how finding your Element can be genuinely transformational in your life. They also illustrate the obstacles and frustrations that most people experience along the way and that are an inevitable part of living real lives.

Exercises

There are practical exercises to help you in finding your Element. You might find some of the exercises more interesting, demanding or revealing than others. It all depends on how you choose to use them and how deeply you want to immerse yourself in them. You can skip over them if you wish. You can read them through quickly and pretend that you've done them. That's up to you. This is your book and your time.

If you're serious about finding your Element, my advice is that you should give all of them a try. They are not tests that you can get wrong or fail. They're not based on a magic formula that guarantees a successful outcome. They're designed to help you think more deeply about your self, your circumstances, your talents, passions, attitudes and possibilities.

Some of these exercises need materials. If you can, get a collection of these together: large sheets of paper, colored pens and pencils, Post-it notes in different colors, a selection of magazines, sticky tape and anything else you'd like to work or play with. As you go through the book, you should also keep a journal and a scrapbook. Use them as often as possible to explore and record your thoughts, images, doodles, drawings, tunes and the like. Make these as varied and multimedia-based as you can.

One of the main themes of this book is that we all think differently. So you should be flexible and creative in how you approach these exercises. The point is to explore them in the ways that you find most revealing. If you're good with words, you may prefer to write. Equally, you may prefer to doodle or draw pictures, or to move or dance or make something with your hands or create diagrams and equations. Whether you prefer to use physical materials or applications on your computer is up to you. Do what works best for you. Whatever that is may be an important clue to your own Element.

Whatever you use, I encourage you to be as focused as possible and to avoid other distractions while you're working on these exercises. For each of them, make time to be on your own for half an hour or so with nothing else to do. If you want to use a computer, turn off everything else that's not relevant—phones, text messages, social media and other applications and programs. Don't worry. It's only half an hour. The digital world will still be there when you turn them all back on again.

Resources

Throughout the book there are suggestions for other resources that you may find helpful. There is, for example, a vast literature on aptitudes, as there is on attitude and personality. There are numerous programs in counseling, personal development and career guidance. Wherever possible, I point to other books and websites that you may find useful and acknowledge other sources that have influenced this book, too. I suggest you look at them not because I endorse them all, but to give you a variety of ways of gathering perspectives on yourself.

Let me add a couple of words of caution. Magazines, newspapers and the Internet are full of quick quizzes and tests that purport to tell you what sort of person you are and what you may be good at. Many people want to believe these tests just as they strain to find personal relevance in general horoscopes that are read by millions of people. Often there's a kernel of truth in them, but you shouldn't try to force yourself into the mold they provide. Finding your Element is about finding yourself.

In 1948, the American psychologist Bertram Forer published the results of research into what he called "subjective validation." Forer gave a personality test to a wide cross-section of his students. Rather than analyzing their responses individually and giving them each a unique evaluation, he gave all of them exactly the same profile that he copied from a newspaper astrology column. He told them that the profile was personal to them and had been tailored to their individual results on the test. Most of these statements could apply to anyone. They were later described as "Barnum statements" after the circus impresario P. T. Barnum, whose sales slogan was "We have something for everyone." This was the profile:

> You have a great need for other people to like and admire you. You have a tendency to be critical of yourself. You have a great deal of unused capacity, which you have not turned to your advantage. While you have some personality weaknesses, you are generally able to compensate for them. Disciplined and self-controlled outside, you tend to be worrisome and insecure inside. At times you have serious doubts as to whether you have made the right decision or done the right thing. You prefer a certain amount of change and variety and become dissatisfied when hemmed in by restrictions and limitations. You pride yourself as an independent thinker and do not accept others' statements without satisfactory proof. You have found it unwise to be too frank in revealing yourself to others. At times you are extroverted, affable, sociable, while at other times you are introverted, wary, reserved. Some of your aspirations tend to be pretty unrealistic. Security is one of your major goals in life.

The students were asked to say how accurately, on a scale of zero to five, the profile applied to them personally. Zero meant it was not accurate at all; five that it was extremely accurate. The average score was 4.26. Since then, the study has been repeated hundreds of times with all sorts of groups, and the average score still comes out around 4.2. One explanation is that when people take such tests, they want the results to be true and they bend their judgments in that direction.

There are lots of illustrations of this tendency and it's not a recent trend. The wonderfully comic novel *Three Men in a Boat*, by Jerome K. Jerome, was published in 1879. In the opening chapter, the hypochondriac hero is worried that he may be sick. He reaches for a medical dictionary to see what might be wrong:

> I idly turned the leaves, and began to indolently study diseases, generally. I forget which was the first distemper I plunged into—some fearful, devastating scourge, I know— and, before I had glanced half down the list of "premonitory symptoms," it was borne in upon me that I had fairly got it. I sat for a while, frozen with horror; and then, in the listlessness of despair, I again turned over the pages. I came to typhoid fever, read the symptoms, discovered that I had typhoid fever, must have had it for months without knowing it. Wondered what else I had got; turned up St. Vitus's Dance, found, as I expected, that I had that too, began to get interested in my case, and determined to sift it to the bottom, and so started alphabetically. . . . I plodded conscientiously through the twenty-six letters, and the only malady I could conclude I had not got was housemaid's knee. . . . There were no more diseases after zymosis, so I concluded there was nothing else the matter with me.

You can see the problem. The questions, exercises and techniques that are suggested in this book are to help you to reflect on your own talents and interests, feelings and attitudes. As you work through them, be as honest with yourself as you can, and avoid being misled by the Barnum effect or wishful thinking. They won't tell you everything you need to know, and some may be more helpful than others. No general tests or exercises can capture all the complexities of your unique abilities and character. Their role is to stimulate your imagination, self-knowledge and sense of possibility. You should try different approaches and decide whether they capture the truth of you. Use them creatively and critically.

Questions

At the end of every chapter, there are several questions—about fifty altogether by the end of the book. They're not a comprehension test or quiz. None of them has a right or wrong answer. They're offered as a framework for your personal reflection on the themes of each chapter and how they apply to you. You may find some of these questions more interesting and relevant than others. As with the exercises, you may want to respond to them in different ways and media, not only in words. My suggestion is that you don't rush ahead and try to answer them all at once, like filling out an application form. Consider them progressively as you come to them, and take your time. You'll have more to reflect on when you've worked on the exercises that precede them. Bear in mind that the book as a whole is not a task to complete but a resource for a process that may begin here but continue long after the final chapter.

A Personal Quest

Finding your Element is a personal quest. A quest is a search. In medieval Europe, knights undertook quests to accomplish a goal that they valued. Quests involve journeys, adventures and risks, and in their nature the outcomes of a quest are uncertain. And they will be for you, too. The quest for your Element is really a two-way journey. It is an inward journey to explore what lies within you; it is an outward journey to explore opportunities in the world around you. The aim of this book is to help you find your way. Whether you fulfill your quest depends on your commitment and fortitude and on how highly you value the possible prize. If you are prepared to do what it takes, I trust you'll find a lot here to help and inspire you.

Although there are ten chapters in the book, *Finding Your Element* is not a ten-step program. I can't guarantee that by the end of Chapter Ten you'll be in your Element. We all start from different places and have our own paths to take. As with any journey of discovery, there is no guarantee that you will find what you're looking for. This book does not tell you which road to take · or which destination to aim for. It offers a guide to the territory and some basic principles and tools to orient you and help you find a path. Although your journey is unique, it need not be solitary. You may find mentors to help you along the way and the company of others who share your Element.

Finding your Element does not mean ignoring the needs of others who may depend on you. It does not mean abandoning all that you do now. It does mean looking hard at yourself and asking if there's more you can do to realize your own talents and passions. It does means asking yourself what's stopping you and what you can do about it.

Some lives are lived without risk or ambition and some are lived as an adventure. Joseph Campbell examined the heroic myths and legends of world cultures throughout history. Writing about the Hero's Journey, he concluded that all heroes face similar challenges. Your quest too will have its challenges and its rewards.

Although no one else has lived your life before, there are signposts from many others who set out before you that can guide your way. In the end, only you will know if you've arrived or if you need to push on to the next horizon—if you've found your Element or if you are still looking for it. Whichever it proves to be, you should never doubt that this is a quest worth undertaking.

Finding Your Element

CHAPTER ONE

Finding Your Element

FINDING YOUR ELEMENT is a highly personal and often surprising process. We are all starting from different places in terms of our own characteristics and circumstances. The Element is also different for each of us. Even so, there are some common principles that underlie this process that apply to everyone, and techniques and strategies that everyone can use. This chapter says what these principles are and why it's important to understand them. It also introduces some initial techniques and exercises to help you take stock of where you are now and to begin to plan the way ahead.

As an example of how curious this process can be, let me start by telling you something about how I came to be doing what I do. I'm often asked what my own Element is and when I knew. Like most others, my story is fairly improbable and it illustrates all of these principles.

I am reasonably good at all sorts of things, most of which I've never pursued. In my teens, I used to tinkle on the piano and I thought I could sense a world-class talent forming deep within me. But when I noticed that real pianists typically play with both hands, I quietly moved on. I could pick out riffs on a guitar and quickly mastered the opening notes of "Whole Lotta Love" by

Led Zeppelin. Then I listened to the rest of the track and decided to leave the field to Jimmy Page. Plus, playing the guitar hurts your fingers.

When I was much younger, I loved drawing and painting but had to drop art at school to focus on other things. As a teenager and into my twenties and thirties, I always liked to fix things and was often to be found in hardware stores admiring routers and drill bits. I also enjoyed cooking and, at one stage when my children were young, had a small but well-deserved reputation for my pastry—at least with them.

In short, from concertos to haute cuisine, I had many options that I might have pursued in my life but did not. Being fairly good at several things, of course, can make it much harder to know what to do with your life than if you are really good at something in particular. I'll come back to that later. The fact is that when I was younger, I had no idea what my Element was, and would not have known even if the phrase had occurred to me at the time, which it had not.

I know now that my Element is communicating and working with people. I've spent a lot of my time traveling around the world presenting to hundreds and often thousands of people, and, through the media, sometimes to millions. When I was very young, I would never have guessed that this would be my Element and nor would anyone who knew me.

I was born in 1950 in Liverpool, England. I grew up in a large, close-knit family that was also tremendously sociable and funny. But as a young child, I spent a lot of time on my own. This was partly circumstance. In the early fifties, Europe and the United States suffered a rampant epidemic of polio. Parents everywhere lived in terror of their children catching the virus. When I was four, I did. Literally overnight, I went from being a strong, fit and highly energetic child, to being almost completely paralyzed. I spent the next eight months in a hospital, some of it in an isolation ward. When I finally came out, I was wearing two leg braces and was in a wheelchair, or walking on crutches.

I have to say that at this point I was almost unbearably cute. I was five years old and in addition to all the orthopedic paraphernalia, I had curly blond hair and a winsome smile that makes my own toes curl now just to think of it. On top of that, I had a pronounced lisp. At breakfast, I might ask for "a cup of tea with two thpoonth of thugar and a peeth of toatht." The net result was that people would melt in my presence and complete strangers would spontaneously offer me money in the street. The lisp was so marked that from the age of three I had weekly sessions with a speech therapist in Liverpool. One theory is that I may have picked up the virus there, since I was the only person among all my family and friends to catch it.

So one reason for spending time on my own was circumstance. Although my family was wonderful in not treating me differently, the fact was that I could not keep up with all the running games in the street or the local park, and I did spend more time on my own than I might otherwise have done. But the other reason was disposition.

As a child I was fairly placid and self-contained. I was a natural observer and listener, and I was happy to sit quietly and take things in from the sidelines. I also loved to make things and solve practical puzzles. At elementary school, one of my favorite lessons was woodwork. I would also spend hours at home assembling and painting plastic models of ships, airplanes and historical figures. I played a lot with Meccano and Legos. I amused myself for whole afternoons in our backyard inventing fantasy games with whatever was lying around. None of this pointed very clearly to a life in the public eye and an international reputation, which I now seem to have, as a public speaker. As is often the case, other people saw my potential before I did.

When I was thirteen, my cousin Brenda got married. Two of my elder brothers, Keith and Ian, and our cousin Billy put together a cabaret act for the evening that involved them dressing up as women and miming to current hit records that were speeded up to sound like Alvin and the Chipmunks. They called themselves The Alka Seltzers. (It's a long story.) They needed someone to introduce them at the event and Keith suggested me. I was astonished, and I wasn't alone in that. But I did do it, even though the idea terrified me.

I was terrified because I'd never done anything remotely like it and because the massed ranks of my Liverpool family are savagely funny and take no prisoners, no matter how many braces and speech impediments are held in front of them. I did it because I've always believed that you have to move toward your fears and not away from them. If you don't exorcise them, they can haunt you long after they should have faded.

As it happens, it was a fantastic evening. I received due acclaim for my small part. The group was a sensation and had invitations to perform at clubs and theaters across the country. They changed their name to The Alka Sisters (to avoid legal action by the popular antacid) and went on to tour for several years and to win a national talent competition. In the meantime, I had a small realization that I could face the public, too.

In high school, I performed in various plays and directed some. By the time I got to college, I had a taste for acting and directing and, although I never sought it, I was often called on to make speeches in debates and to make presentations. Once I was on stage, I found that I relaxed fairly quickly and enjoyed it. I still do. My professional work has always involved working with and presenting to groups of people. Although I was always nervous beforehand, I found from the beginning that I settled in quickly, and that the time passed quickly while I was doing this.

When you're in your Element, your sense of time changes. If you're doing something that you love, an hour can feel like five minutes; if you are doing something that you do not, five minutes can feel like an hour. At every stage of my working life, my wife, Thérèse, has always said that she can tell at the end of the day what I've been doing. If I've been sitting through routine committee meetings or doing administration, I look ten years older than I am: if I've been speaking at an event, teaching or running a workshop, I look ten years younger. Being in your Element gives you energy. Not being in it takes it from you. We'll talk more about energy in chapter five.

So how do you set about finding *your* Element?

A Two-Way Journey

Finding your Element is a quest to find yourself. As I said in the introduction, it is a two-way journey: an inward journey to explore what lies within you and an outward journey to explore opportunities in the world around you.

You live as we all do in two worlds. There is the world that came into being when you did, and that exists only because you exist. This is the inner world of your personal consciousness: of your own feelings, thoughts, moods and sensations. There is also the world that exists whether or not you exist. This is the external world of other people, of events, of circumstances and material things. This outer world was there long before you were born, and it will continue long after you have left it. You only know the outer world through your inner world. You perceive it through your physical senses and you make sense of it through the ideas, values, feelings and attitudes that make up your worldview.

To find your Element, you have to explore both of these worlds. You need to fathom your own talents and passions and you need to look creatively at opportunities in the world around you to fulfill them. In practical terms, finding your Element involves three processes. You should try to practice each of them regularly because each will feed the other.

Turn Down the Noise

To find your Element you have to get to know yourself better. You have to spend time with yourself, apart from other people's opinions of you. For many of us, this is easier said than done.

Few of us choose to live in total isolation from the rest of humanity. In the ordinary course of your life, you probably spend most of your time with other people—family and neighbors, friends and acquaintances and the people you work with. There are the few people you know intimately and the many that you know only in passing and all the ones in between. As you get older, you accumulate responsibilities and take on new roles. In any given day, you may switch between all of them, perhaps as a parent, as friend, lover or partner, as a student, a teacher, a breadwinner or dependent. Like everyone else, you are bound to be affected by how other people see you and by how you want to be seen by them—by what they want for you and what they expect from you.

We also live in times of tremendous "noise" and distraction. The world is becoming increasingly turbulent. It is difficult, for example, to overstate the impact of digital technologies on how we think, live and work. The benefits of these technologies are extraordinary, but there are drawbacks, too. One of them is trying to keep up with the flood of information that pours through our televisions, laptops, tablets and smart phones. In 2010, Eric Schmidt, CEO of Google, estimated that every two days we now create as much information as we did from the dawn of civilization up until 2003. According to researchers at Cisco Systems, by the end of 2010 the amount of data traveling across the Internet was equivalent to the information contained on a bookshelf thirty-six billion miles long (ten times the distance from Earth to Pluto). Every five minutes, it's estimated that we create a "blizzard of digital data" equivalent to all of the information stored in the U.S. Library of Congress. Maybe. Estimates vary.

For all of their benefits, these technologies tend to draw us constantly outward to the external world rather than toward what lies within us. They may also encourage rapid responses rather than deep engagement and critical reflection.

When you add the noise of the external world to all the roles you take in it, it is easy to lose sight of who you really are. To find your Element, you need to regain that perspective. One way is to create time and space to be alone with yourself, to experience who you are when no one else wants anything from you and the noise has stopped. One method is to meditate.

I say this with some hesitation. Frankly, I am not very good at meditating. I do try it and I do my best, but I have a short attention span and I am habitually restless. When I was growing up, my dad was always telling me to stop fidgeting. I never did. Now that I am a dad, my own family is always trying to get me to meditate. To paraphrase Dr. Johnson, the renowned eighteenth-century author and wit, to see me meditate "is like a dog walking on its hind legs. It is not done well, but you are surprised to find it done at all." When I do meditate privately, I make a point of telling everyone I've been doing it, which probably defeats the purpose.

In fairness to me, meditation is more difficult than its popular image suggests. At first glance it all seems simple enough. Meditation is a process of calming your mind and dwelling in the quiet flow of your own being. It is a way of easing the outer world's expectations of you and allowing your essential self to breathe and to be.

The most common challenge in meditation is to stop thinking, which turns out to be one of the reasons for doing it. Meditation is not thinking. In some ways, it is the opposite. In the West we tend to equate intelligence with having organized thoughts. Thinking has some obvious benefits and in general I am all for it. In fact, when you are not meditating, I strongly encourage you to do it. I wish some people would think more. But thinking is not the same as consciousness. We'll come back to this, too, in chapter five. Sometimes, as Eckhart Tolle says in *The Power of Now*, thinking too much can limit our consciousness.

If you're anything like me and most people I know, the ordinary experience of your mind is probably a constant chattering of thoughts and feelings. This internal cacophony can be like white noise on a television screen that interferes with the underlying signal. One of the aims of meditation is to reduce this mental static so that you can experience deeper levels of consciousness. An ancient analogy compares the turbulence of the thinking mind with the waves and ripples on the surface of a lake. It is only by calming the disturbed surface that you can see into the depths that lie beneath.

I am willing to admit that I find meditation difficult because many people do. If it were so easy to stop thinking there would be no need to think about how to do it. The good news is that there are many ways to meditate. Some practices require mystical settings and improbable positions. Others do not. For some people, yoga is the best way. For others, simply taking time to breathe, relax and be quiet with themselves is enough to begin with.

Before each of the practical exercises in this book, I suggest that you try a simple meditation just for a few minutes, to calm yourself and focus on the questions you're going to explore. Here's one way to do this:

Exercise One: Meditation

- If you can, sit comfortably with your back and shoulders straight but relaxed. Close your eyes.
- Take a deep breath through your nose, hold it for a few seconds and slowly let it out.
- As you do, try to focus your attention on the flow of your breath. Repeat this slowly four or five times.
- Then breathe normally for a few minutes and try to keep focused on the feeling of your breathing.
- As random thoughts come into mind—and they inevitably will—don't try to stop them. Keep your focus on your breath, relax and just be.
- After five minutes or so—ten if you can manage it—open your eyes and relax quietly for another couple of minutes.

Although I struggle with meditation myself, I do recommend that you try a number of different approaches and see what works best for you. As easily distracted as we are, even a few minutes each day can be a powerful way of reconnecting with yourself and brightening your sense of who you are beneath the surface. Like most things that are worth doing, it is not easy but it does reward you in the end.

Change Your Perspective

To find your Element, you may need to see yourself differently. The poet Anaïs Nin once said, "I don't see the world as it is: I see it as I am." She meant that no one has a neutral point of view. We see the world around us from the world within us and each shapes our perspective on the other. As human beings, we do not always see the world directly; we interpret our experiences through patterns of ideas, values and beliefs. Some of these have to do with our own dispositions and some have to do with the cultures we're part of and the times we live in. In all areas of our lives, whether and how we act is affected by how we think and feel. Your own attitudes and those of the people around you may help or hinder you in finding what your Element is and pursuing it.

Let's start with your own assumptions. You may think, for example, that you have no special aptitudes. Many people think that until they discover that they do and what these are. You may think that you have no passions; many people think that too and then find that they have. You may have told yourself for a long time that you're not good at something that you would love to try and so you haven't. Or you may be worried that if you do try you'll fail and look foolish. Or you may think that the moment has passed to try something new. All of these stories that you tell yourself about yourself can stand between you and finding your Element.

Finding your Element may mean challenging other people's assumptions about what you're capable of doing. You may have absorbed attitudes about yourself from friends and family that you've just come to accept. You also live as part of a wider culture, which has its own ways of thinking and of doing things. Certain options may be discouraged or frowned upon within that culture, according to your age or gender or your existing roles and responsibilities.

We'll consider all of these issues as we go on. My point here is that in order to discover what your Element is, you may need to challenge ideas about yourself that you and others have come to take for granted. Reflecting on your own natural aptitudes and on the experiences that you have been most drawn to in the past and on those that you'd like to explore in future is an essential part of finding your Element. Some of the exercises in this book are designed to help you to do this. As you work through them, you can use many different modes of reflection: words, images, sounds, movement and all the many ways in which they combine. Here are three techniques that you may find especially helpful.

Mind Mapping

Mind mapping is a visual technique for displaying or sorting information. A mind map centers on a core idea or theme and has lines, words and images extending from it to connecting ideas or information. To create a mind map, you begin by putting the core idea or theme in the center of the page and draw a circle around it. You then draw branching lines from the center circle that represent related thoughts and ideas. You can have as many of these branching lines as you like and each of them may divide into two or more other lines of thought.

As an example of this technique, here's a simple mind map of the structure and main themes of this book:

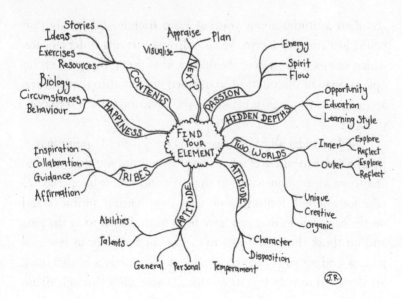

The originator of the modern mind map is Tony Buzan. He and his brother Barry Buzan cowrote *The Mind Map*, which is probably the best guide to this technique. There are also many examples and guidelines on the Internet, which should help and inspire you. There is no wrong way to create a mind map as long as it makes sense to you. Mind mapping offers you a lot of creative freedom and can open whole new ways of thinking. Here are some of the main principles you should keep in mind as you practice mind mapping:

- Use single words or very short phrases for each line. Remember, this is a visual as much as a verbal system.
- Use uppercase letters for key words and upper- and lowercase for others.
- Each key word or image should have its own line.

- Make the lines the same length as the word/image they support.
- Make the lines flowing and curving rather than straight and angular. One of the aims of a mind map is to form organic connections.
- As they radiate from the center the lines should be thicker to begin with then become thinner as they branch into subsidiary and related themes.
- Use a variety of colors throughout the mind map. Colors give the map visual appeal and they help to identify different levels and types of ideas.

You'll have noticed, no doubt, that our mind map of the book does not use color or images and that it's fairly simple. That's because we want this one to illustrate the basic principles of a mind map. The other reason is that by keeping it in black and white, we're saving you money on color printing. We thought you'd like that. Now that you have the book, though, feel free to color it in yourself! It will be good practice.

Vision Boards

A vision board is a collage of images that reflect your aspirations, hopes and dreams. Vision boards are a great way of sorting through what you hope to create in your life and "putting it out there." Creating a vision board can be a relaxing, therapeutic and really enjoyable process.

To make a vision board, sift through a selection of magazines that relate to your interests, hobbies and passions and cut out images, pictures and phrases that speak to you. You can also look online. Personal photographs are a bit more complicated as they are representative of the past, not the future, so I would recommend avoiding them for this particular exercise.

Once you have your selection of images you have a few options. For the most common form of vision board, you glue or tape your pictures onto a large piece of poster board. While this is a great medium for display, I recommend using something less permanent than glue or tape to attach your images. As you continue on your journey to finding your Element, and even after having discovered it, your hopes and dreams may change. You may start off this journey with a clear image of what you want to achieve and stick to it throughout. Similarly, you may not, and you'll want to be able to adjust your vision board accordingly. To allow you to make changes, I recommend using pushpins, Velcro or tacky glue. You don't have to use a piece of cardboard. Corkboards are great, too. Some people use mirrors with magnets for their boards, or even windows. Get creative here.

What you do with your completed vision board is entirely a matter of personal choice and circumstance. There is a lot to be said for keeping your vision board on display so you see it during your regular day-to-day activities. If you feel your board is private and personal, keep it out of view from others but where you can easily look at it as often as you would like. The main purpose of creating a vision board is to create a clear visualization of the life you would like to lead, so have fun with this exercise and focus on making it a true representation of you. Do not give in to other influences. You are creating a vision of your life, not someone else's.

Automatic Writing

The idea behind both vision boards and mind maps is to encourage you to think visually and associatively, rather than only in words or in linear sequences. By disrupting your normal patterns of thought you may see yourself in new ways. You can do this with words too, of course, especially if you practice writing freely just for yourself, without judgment or self-consciousness. One technique for doing this is automatic writing.

The aim of automatic writing is to explore your thoughts and feelings in a spontaneous, unplanned and uncensored way without consciously controlling what you're writing. Rather than setting out to present an organized point of view to yourself or anyone else, you simply start writing what comes first to your consciousness and move in any direction you like through a process of free association. You don't pause to correct or judge what you're writing or to plan what you might write next. As with vision boards, you're gathering impressions and feelings, and as with mind maps, you're free to make whatever connections occur to you in the process.

To practice automatic writing, be somewhere you can relax with a good supply of paper of whatever size and color appeals to you and something you feel comfortable writing with. Think for a moment of what the issue, question or theme is that you want to explore. Let's say the keywords are "my passions." Without thinking any further, just start to write whatever comes first to you. Try to keep up a steady flow of writing for five minutes or so, without stopping to change or amend. As you practice, you'll find that you'll write for longer without pausing. It may help to give yourself a time limit during each session of ten, fifteen or twenty minutes. Don't worry about spelling and punctuation or format. The purpose is to get your thoughts and feelings on the page as freely as possible. The result isn't for anyone but you—unless you choose to share it. It's a process of spontaneous, uninterrupted personal expression. When you've finished and feel ready, read through what you've written. You might circle whatever phrases or words strike you as especially significant and take one or more of those as the starting point for your next piece of automatic writing. Another technique is to take each letter of the keyword (p-a-s-s-i-o-n) as random starting points.

In her best-selling book *The Artist's Way*, Julia Cameron recommends starting every day with automatic writing for what she calls Morning Pages. Rather than being focused on anything in particular, Morning Pages are a way of clearing the clutter from your consciousness before you start the day. As Julia Cameron describes them, "Morning Pages are three pages of longhand, stream-of-consciousness writing, done first thing in the morning. There is no wrong way to do Morning Pages—they are not high art. They are about anything and everything that crosses your mind—and they are for your eyes only. Occasionally colorful, more often than not Morning Pages are negative, fragmented, repetitive or bland. Good! Worrying about your job, the laundry, the weird look your friend gave you—all that stuff distracts you from your creativity. It eddies through your sub-consciousness and muddies your day. Get it on the page first thing in the morning and move on with your day with a freer spirit."

Cameron recommends that you write your Morning Pages first thing in the morning, before you do anything else. You need to have a notebook or pieces of paper and a pen near to your bed so that as soon as you wake up they are within easy reach. Next, you write. Julia Cameron is clear about writing three pages, or for twenty minutes, whichever comes first. In the case of Morning Pages, she also recommends that you don't read them again so that what you have just written doesn't come flooding back into your mind. She has even suggested shredding them once you are finished. If you hesitate to shred them, she suggests keeping them in a large envelope out of reach of others. You could also write all of your pages in one notebook and hide that. Whichever method you choose, Morning Pages are a great way of clearing your mind for the day, allowing you to focus on what's to come.

Give It a Try

To find out what lies within, you also have to look outside yourself. You need to try new activities, visit new places and meet new people. You need to put yourself in the way of new opportunities and test yourself in different circumstances. If there are activities or experiences you have wanted to try, you should try them. If there are things that you have been anxious about doing, but feel intrigued by them, you should try them. If you don't try new things then you may never find out what you are capable of.

Of course, you cannot do everything. Part of the purpose of meditating and reflecting is to identify the experiences that matter most for you and find out how to make them possible. As we go on through the book, there are also exercises and tasks to help you look outward and clarify the directions in which you might begin to move.

Circumstances matter and so do your personal background and life experiences so far. But whatever your situation, in the end, it's not what happens to you that makes the biggest difference in your life, it's what you make of what happens that matters most.

Getting Started

Stopping the noise, changing perspective, and giving it a try are three core processes for finding your Element. You could treat them as one-off events if you like and just do them once. But if you're serious about finding your Element, I suggest that you don't. It would be like trying to get in good physical shape by working out once and assuming you've done all that's needed. Like getting and staying in shape, these three processes are part of a continuing cycle of focus, exploration and reflection, the aim of which is to deepen your understanding of yourself and the world around you. Let's start that cycle with this next exercise.

Exercise Two: What Are You Doing?

The aim of this exercise is to help you take stock of where you are now in your life and what you feel about it:

- On a large sheet of paper, make a list of keywords or collect some images of all the things you do in a typical week. They might include meetings, e-mails, cleaning, shopping, socializing, commuting, studying, surfing the Internet, listening to music, gardening, watching movies, paying bills, working out, babysitting. Everyone's life is different. So what's in yours?
- Using different colors, highlight activities that you would naturally group together. The categories might include, for example, paid work, unpaid work, recreation, socializing, hobbies, keeping fit. Use whatever categories make the most sense to you.
- On a second piece of paper, draw separate circles for each of these broad categories. Make the circles roughly equal to how much time you spend on each of them each week. If you work three times more than you relax, the work

circle should be three times as big. Put in each of the circles all the keywords or images for that category.

- Now think about how you feel about all of these things that you do. Do you love your work but not working out? Do you love socializing but not studying? Using three different colors, highlight each item according to whether:

  a) you like it,

  b) don't mind it,

  c) don't like it.

- On a new sheet of paper, draw one large circle and divide it roughly into three segments to show how much time you spend on what you like, don't mind or dislike doing. How's it looking? How would the pie slice for a month, or a year?

Spend a little time reflecting on the pattern of your life that this exercise has shown. What do you feel about it? What flexibility do you see here? What would you like to change? Why is that? What can you change now and what will take you longer to work out? Do you have a sense of where you would like to get to? It doesn't matter now if you don't. We're coming to that shortly.

Before we move on and build on these first exercises, let me introduce and explain the principles I mentioned that underpin this whole process.

Three Elemental Principles

I said earlier that finding your Element is not a ten-step program. It is a highly personal process that has different outcomes for all of us. That's true. But the process itself is based on three *elemental* principles that apply to everyone. Here they are.

PRINCIPLE #1: YOUR LIFE IS UNIQUE

Your life is unique in the whole of history. No one has ever lived it before and nobody else ever will. If you are a parent of two or more children, I'll make you a bet. My bet is that they are completely different from each other. You would never mistake them, would you? "Which one are you? Remind me." Even identical twins are different in many ways. I'll make the same bet if you have any siblings or relatives. I am one of seven children, and we are all different. Of course we are alike in some respects, and we all love each other, but we all have our own quirks, interests and temperaments. My wife and I have two children and they are very alike in some ways and like chalk and cheese in others. As the dancer Martha Graham put it, "There is a vitality, a life force, an energy, a quickening, that is translated through you into action and because there is only one of you in all time, that expression is unique."

You are unique in two ways. The first is biological.

Although your life is unique, it was taking shape long before you were born. It's worth remembering that the odds against your being born in the first place were extremely high. Think, for example, about how many human beings have ever lived. I do not mean prehistoric creatures that walked on their knuckles. I mean modern human beings like us, with attractive profiles and a sense of irony. Our own species, Homo sapiens, is thought to have emerged on Earth about fifty to one hundred thousand years ago. How many human lives do you think there have there been down these five hundred centuries or so?

As it happens, nobody really knows, because nobody has been counting, at least not until very recently. Any answer is bound to be a very rough estimate. Even so, statisticians have tried to come to a reasonable estimate that takes account of birth and mortality rates, life spans, and so on down the ages. The best estimates seem to be somewhere between sixty and a hundred-and-ten billion. Let's split the difference and say that maybe eighty billion human beings have drawn breath since the dawn of human history.

Think of how you actually came to be one of those eighty billion. Think of the fine threads of your own ancestry that wove through all the generations of humanity and led to your own birth and life. Think of how many people down all of those centuries had to meet each other and have lives and children of their own until eventually your own great grandparents were born— all eight of them. Think about how they met and how, through them, your four grandparents were born and met and then gave birth to your two parents who eventually gave birth to you. When you consider all the chance meetings, random introductions, and blind dates that happened along the way, being born at all, as the Dalai Lama once said, is a miracle.

I say that your life was taking shape long before you were born because you carry within you the biological memories of all your forebears. As Judith Butler puts it, "I am not fully known to myself because part of what I am is the enigmatic traces of others." These traces have influenced how you look, your gender, your ethnicity and your sexuality. They have also affected your natural constitution, aptitudes and personality. I'm very like my father, for example. I look like him and I'm like him in temperament. Many of the characteristics that I might think of as particular to me I've inherited from him and so, in different ways, have my brothers and my wonderful sister, Rob. Even so, we are not clones of him. We also share other characteristics that we inherited from our mother. And both of our parents owed much of who they were to our grandparents, and so do we. Each of us combines these and other personal characteristics in our own unique ways.

Learning more about your own genetic inheritance can be a powerful way of understanding why you think and feel as you do. Tracing the path that led you here can also help to reveal the way ahead. *Finding your Element involves understanding the powers and passions that you were born with as part of your unique biological inheritance.*

The second reason that you are unique is cultural. When communities create shared ideas, values and patterns of behavior, they create a culture. What you make of what lies within you is affected by the culture you are part of: by what it encourages and discourages, permits or forbids. Whether you find your Element may be affected by whether you live in poverty or prosperity, in peace or war, and by what sort of education you have, if any. One of the reasons why my life is not identical with that of my parents is that I was born into different times and circumstances. My father was born in 1914 and my mother in 1919, both in Liverpool. Although I was born in Liverpool too, the world of their childhood and adolescence in the 1920s and 1930s was unrecognizably different from the one in which I grew up in the 1950s and 1960s.

Our own lives are all shaped by the crosscurrents of our personalities and the circumstances in which we live. The decisions you make and that others make for you all influence the paths you take or turn away from. *Finding your Element means reflecting on your own cultural circumstances—on the opportunities for growth that you want and need now.*

PRINCIPLE #2: YOU CREATE YOUR OWN LIFE

Whatever your history and circumstances, you should never feel locked in by what has happened to you up to now. It is often said that you cannot change the past but you can change the future. And so you can, because of your very nature as a human being.

In most respects we are like the rest of life on Earth. We are mortal and depend on the Earth for our survival. We are organic: we grow and change as other living things do. But in one critical respect, we are completely different.

Human beings appeared on Earth about fifty to one hundred thousand years ago. That seems like a long time—and it is—but in terms of the life of the planet, it is the beat of a wing. The Earth itself is thought to be about four-and-a-half billion years old. This is an inconceivably long time. If you were to imagine that whole period as a single year, modern human beings appeared on Earth at about one minute to midnight on December 31st. For most of our time here, we lived harmoniously with the rest of nature. In the last three hundred years, we have come to dominate it in many ways. Why is this? What has set human beings apart from the rest of nature? The short answer, I believe, is that human beings have immense natural powers of imagination and creativity.

Imagination is the ability to bring to mind things that are not present to our senses. In imagination you can step outside the present moment and look back to the past. In imagination, you can enter other people's inner worlds and try to see with their eyes and feel what they are feeling. You can empathize. In imagination, you can anticipate the future and try to bring it about. These powers of hindsight, empathy and foresight are among your best resources in shaping and reshaping your own life.

Imagination is the source of creativity. Creativity is about putting your imagination to work. It is applied imagination. It is from our collective powers of creativity that the most important human achievements have flowed: in the arts and sciences, in all the languages we speak, the technologies we make, and in the ideas and cultural values we believe in.

In a biological sense, we are probably evolving at the same rate as other species. But culturally, we are in a different class. Dogs have been around for a long time too, but they have not changed much in how they live and what interests them. I am not saying that dogs do not have imaginations; I do not know. But they don't manifest them as we do and they are not evolving culturally very quickly as a result. They are still getting by much as they did in ancient times. You don't need to keep checking in with dogs to see what is new.

With people there's always something new. The reason is that human beings are naturally creative. This is true of us as a species and of our individual lives. You create your own life by how you see the world and your place in it; by the opportunities you take and the ones you refuse; by the possibilities you see and the choices you make. As a human being, you have many choices. For you, if not necessarily for your dog, imagination and creativity come with the kit.

You're not given your résumé with your birth certificate. You create your life and you can recreate it. As the psychologist George Kelly says, "No one needs to be a victim of their own biography." Or, as Carl Jung puts it, "I am not what has happened to me, I am what I choose to become."

PRINCIPLE #3: LIFE IS ORGANIC

In my experience, very few people in middle age or beyond correctly anticipated the lives they have actually led. Even if they're doing generally what they had in mind, and few are, they could not have foreseen all the nuances: this job, this partner, these homes and, if they have them, these children. How could they? I include myself in this.

There was a time when I might have been a dentist or an accountant. When I was about to leave high school, I met the careers teacher. It was the only time we did meet. He asked me what I enjoyed most in school and I told him English, Latin and French. I loved French. Actually, I loved the French teacher, Mr. Evans. To begin with, he could actually speak French, which was not the case with all French teachers. He was also young and suave, which was absolutely not the case with all of them. And he smoked French cigarettes and ate garlic, which in 1960s England was tremendously exotic. I used to think garlic was a drug. Part of me still does. Food in Britain then was generally less cosmopolitan—and less edible—than it is now. I was twenty before I saw a zucchini and in my mid-twenties before I encountered an eggplant. I still wish I hadn't. On top of all of that, Mr. Evans had a French wife. We couldn't imagine it. Actually we could and we spent most of our French lessons doing exactly that.

With a touching confidence in my careers teacher's grasp of human nature and the mysteries of the future, I waited to hear what path through life my interests in French, Latin and English would reveal to him. He thought for a moment and then asked if I'd thought of being an accountant. I had not. A dentist? Again, no. I had overlooked both options. As it happens, neither of us anticipated the life I went on to have, which has had absolutely

nothing to do with numbers or with cavities, except my own, and
very little to do with French.

The reason that neither he nor I could predict my life, any
more than you can predict yours, is that life is not linear; it is organic. My life, like yours, is a constant process of improvisation
between my interests and personality on the one hand and circumstances and opportunities on the other. The one affects the
other. Many of the opportunities you have in your life are gener-
ated by the energy you create around you.

Of course, the whole process can seem very different when
you come to write your résumé. You then impose a linear narra-
tive on your life, to make it look as if it was all planned and delib-
erate. You organize your story around key dates and achievements,
with headings in bold and italic, to give the impression that your
life has been unfolding according to a sensible, premeditated
scheme. You do this to encourage yourself and to avoid giving
prospective employers the impression that your life has been the
uncertain process of tacking and weaving that most lives really are.

There are many examples throughout this book of lives that
illustrate the truth of these three principles. Take the career of
David Ogilvy, sometimes called the "Father of Advertising." It
was the work of Ogilvy's agency in New York in the sixties that
inspired the hit TV series *Mad Men*. Given his legendary success
on Madison Avenue, you might assume that he was born in
America, spent his whole life in advertising and never wanted to
do anything else. You would be wrong.

David Ogilvy was born in 1911 in England. He was educated
in Edinburgh and at Oxford. He started his career as a chef in the
Hotel Majestic in Paris. He went on to sell cooking stoves in Scotland. Because he was so good at this, he was asked by the owner of
the company to write a sales manual for the other salesmen. It was

published and was described thirty years later by *Fortune* magazine as the best sales manual ever written by anybody. His older brother, Francis, showed the manual to executives at the London advertising agency Mather and Crowley, where he was working. They were so impressed that they offered David a junior position there. After a successful stint, David moved to America to become an associate director of Gallup, the social survey organization. During World War II, he was appointed to the staff of British Intelligence Services at the British embassy in Washington, D.C.

He decided to leave the city altogether when the war ended, and joined an Amish community on the East Coast of America to become a farmer. Then, after ten years on the land, he decided to head back to New York to join the Mather advertising agency as an account executive. Over the next twenty years, he turned it into the world's leading agency, which was aptly renamed Ogilvy Mather. All as the night follows the day, so to speak. It's a familiar story: from stove salesman in Scotland, to Amish farmer, to global executive on Madison Avenue. Ogilvy's life is a striking example of how we create our own lives from many disparate elements—of how life is not linear, it is organic.

Finding your Element means being open to new experiences and to exploring new paths and possibilities in yourself and in the world around you.

True North

Let me say a quick word about education. One of the problems you may face in finding your Element is that most systems of education are not based on the three elemental principles—your life is unique, you create your life, your life is organic. On the contrary. For the most part education systems inhibit creativity and are organized on the false assumptions that life is linear and inorganic. The conventional story is that if you study particular disciplines and stay with the prescribed program, and pass all the tests, your life will fall neatly into place. If you don't, it won't.

Well, it might work that way, according to how sure you are of what you want to do. Then again, it might not. For example, there is often no direct relationship between what you study in school and the work you do when you leave and the life you may go on to lead. You might imagine, for example, that engineers dominate companies in Silicon Valley and that there is a strong connection between innovation in these companies and leaders who specialize in mathematics and science. You would be wrong. Vivek Wadhwa is a professor at the Pratt School of Engineering at Duke University. He surveyed more than six hundred and fifty U.S.-born CEOs and heads of product engineering at more than five hundred technology companies. Just over ninety percent of them had college degrees. Of those, only four out of ten had degrees in engineering or math. The other sixty percent had degrees in business, the arts or the humanities.

Professor Wadhwa concluded that there is no link between what you study in college and how successful or otherwise you are later in your life. He has been involved in hiring more than a thousand people and has found no relation between the field of study and success in the workplace. "What makes people successful," he said, "are their motivation, drive, and ability to learn from mistakes and how hard they work." It is important to emphasize this principle because young people are often steered away from courses they would like to take in school by well-meaning parents, friends or teachers who tell them they will never get a job doing that. Real life often tells a different story.

Katharine Brooks is director of Liberal Arts Career services at the University of Texas at Austin. She says that most students are encouraged to think that career planning is logical and linear: "I majored in political science, so I'll go to law school" or "I studied history so I'll be a history teacher." In fact, many—perhaps a majority—of people move in completely different directions once they cast off from college and set sail in the world. Most graduates then discover that they are actually interested in other things. She estimates that less than a third of the alumni who stay in touch with her are in careers that are directly related to their college studies.

What about this majority who discover other interests? Are they happy? They are if they are fulfilling their passions. "The saddest thing to me," says Dr. Brooks, "is seeing someone take the job because it pays well and then spend all that money on toys to cheer themselves up for being so miserable in their jobs. The people who are doing what they love hardly feel they're working at all, just living."

My careers teacher did not help me because he was not really looking at me; he was looking at a general list of occupations and trying to fit me into it. Even so, it's hard to understand his leap of imagination from what I said I enjoyed to the careers he suggested. But at least he had some ideas for what I should do. I did not. I had only a vague plan to study English literature. I also had a general sense of what I wanted to avoid. I was drawn more to the arts than to the sciences. I didn't see myself going into management or administrative work. I did like putting on plays and I liked working with people, especially if they were funny. I was not drawn to working in the theater. As it happens, this vague sense of orientation was all I really needed. I'll come back later to what I actually did do. I think of this general orientation as trying to find your own True North.

Everyone has their own starting points. Some people have a

clear vision of where they want to be years from now. They have goals that act like beacons on the horizon and guide their steps. Others have only a vague feeling that they're currently heading in the wrong direction. What about you? Having a general sense of direction does not commit you to anything but it does help to give you some initial reference points. It can also help you choose between different paths, some of which you may already know intuitively do not interest you. Are there some things that you can see yourself doing with your life and others that you really cannot? You may have a very clear sense of direction. Equally you may not. So let's take a look at that.

Exercise Three: Picture Yourself

Look back at the pattern of your life that you mapped out in Exercise Two. Make a visual collage of your life. Don't use photographs or images of people you actually know personally. The aim is to represent the general pattern of things you do and to capture your general outlook and feelings about your life as it is now:

- Look through a range of magazines. Cut out images, headlines or words that appeal to you for whatever reason.
- Select from these images any that represent some aspect of your current life. Use images that capture the activities you engage in and whether you enjoy them or just get through them.
- Arrange them in a pattern in any way that captures for you the character and feel of your current life.
- Feel free to write and doodle on the images. Customize them any way that feels right to capture the mood of what you're expressing.

- If you have the technology and inclination, you could also add your own soundtrack.
- Ask yourself how well this representation of your life expresses your feelings and experiences. Which areas do you feel happiest with and which ones do you want to focus on changing or improving as you look for your Element?

Charting Your Course

I said earlier that all of our lives are subject to powerful crosscurrents that we cannot always predict and control. That is true. But it's also true that what matters most is how we respond to them. To that extent, living our lives is like steering a ship on the open seas. You can set a course and be determined to stick with it, and some people do. You can also be blown off course by circumstances that you hadn't planned on at all. Some people founder for a while and some do sink. Equally, you may arrive on unexpected shores that prove to be far more interesting than the destination you had in mind. Then you meet new people and have new experiences; you influence them and they affect you and together you change the story of one another's lives. This is especially true when you follow your true talents and passions.

Because life is creative and organic, you do not need to plan your whole life's journey in one go. Sometimes it's helpful to have long-term goals, and some people do. It can be just as helpful to focus on the immediate next steps. Beginning the journey, and being willing to explore various pathways, can be as productive as setting out with a final destination in mind. Sometimes you can only plan the next step. But that can be enough to move forward. The important step is the first one. You need to begin: to set sail.

The philosopher Teilhard de Chardin also used the metaphor

of the ocean as a way of thinking about life's journey. He offered this encouragement: "Instead of standing on the shore and convincing ourselves that the ocean cannot carry us, let us venture onto its waters—just to see."

Here are some questions for you to consider before you move on to the next chapter:

- What have been the most important influences and turning points in your life?
- Which aspects of your life engage you most?
- Which ones engage you least?
- Do you know what your Element is?
- Do you know what direction you want to move in?
- What would you like to do that you haven't tried yet?
- Why haven't you?

CHAPTER TWO

What Are You Good At?

B EING IN YOUR Element is where your natural aptitudes meet your passions. In this chapter, we focus on your aptitudes. We'll get to your passions later. Understanding your own aptitudes is an essential part of finding your Element. One reason that so many people have not found their Element is that they don't know what their aptitudes are. So what are aptitudes and how do you discover yours?

Aptitudes have to do with your biological constitution. They are the natural talents that you were born with. Some aptitudes may show themselves early in your life; others may stay hidden because the opportunity to draw on them never arises.

Even as a child, my elder brother Derek was very good with engines. By the time he was ten, he was stripping down motorcycles to find out how they worked. I could have done that, too. The advantage in his approach was that he could put them back together again and they worked better than before. Our eldest brother, Keith, relied on Derek to keep his own motorbike in peak condition. So did all of Keith's friends and many other people in the part of Liverpool where we lived. By the time he was thirteen Derek was fixing automobile engines. He just gets engines. He can listen to them like a horse whisperer, diagnose the problem and understand the solution. He also spent hours drawing accurate technical diagrams of engines. He had an encyclopedic knowledge of brands and models and a dazzling memory for detail. He still does. He has a natural aptitude for how things work.

You've probably found in your own life that some things you do come easily to you and others do not. We're all the same in this respect. There are activities and processes that we're naturally good at and others that we struggle with. You may be naturally good at sports or have a flair for making things and using tools. The first time you saw a screwdriver lying around you knew instinctively that you were meant to do something with it other than stick it in the nearest electrical outlet. Not everybody does, by the way. My brother Keith has no rapport at all with tools or with fixing things. On the contrary, his rare attempts at putting up shelves or fixing electric appliances have all proved to be near-death experiences. He has his own strengths, though. He's wonderful with people, tremendously funny and a natural performer. You may be too. Or you may be naturally at home with numbers, or with wind instruments or animals. Or not. The first time you needed to take charge of something, you may have slipped into the role without hesitation. When you walk into a room you may immediately see ways to make it feel more open, elegant or brighter.

My wife, Thérèse, does that. She has a natural flair for color, design and texture. She can keep a color in her mind indefinitely and match it perfectly with another piece of fabric, furniture or paint that she sees months later. I cannot. I need to be told what to wear and when. If I'm traveling alone, she helps me pack infallible combinations of shirts, ties and suits that she maintains are impossible to mismatch. She is wrong. Left to my own devices, I reliably find the one improbable combination that doesn't work and then appear in public, proudly sporting my selection to the quiet distress no doubt of those who understand these things.

Aptitudes and Abilities

There is a difference between aptitudes and abilities. Aptitudes are part of your raw potential. To realize that potential, you need to apply and refine them. For example, human beings have a natural aptitude for language. But learning to speak is a cultural process that depends on being exposed to other speakers, especially in infancy. If young children are deprived of human company in their formative years, they don't learn to speak despite their latent aptitude to do so. It's the same with reading and writing. In ordinary circumstances, everyone has the necessary aptitudes for literacy. But many children and adults can't read or write. They're not incapable of reading and writing; they simply haven't learned how to do it. You don't become literate just by getting older. Literacy, like speech, is a cultural achievement. So too is musical ability.

Abilities often require a considerable amount of education and apprenticeship to develop. Just because you have a natural proclivity toward something doesn't mean you'll automatically be expert at it. Having a natural understanding of what to do with a screwdriver doesn't make you a master carpenter. Grasping math quickly doesn't make you an engineer. Having a good visual sense doesn't make you a competent designer. When people say they are good at something ("I'm good at puzzles"), they are often identifying an aptitude. When they define themselves by something ("I'm a cryptographer"), they are usually identifying abilities.

Being in your Element takes both aptitude and ability. It involves finding your natural talents and honing them in practice: it is a union of nature and nurture. It may take much less effort to become good at something that comes naturally to you than at something that doesn't, but if you don't make that effort, you'll never know what you might have achieved if you'd persevered. This was my experience with the guitar and the piano. I have an aptitude for both, but never made the effort to become proficient in them. All of this is good news for Jimmy Page, of course. But for my lack of application he might not be enjoying the unchallenged status that he does today.

General and Personal Aptitudes

You can think of your aptitudes as both general and personal. As human beings we are all born with more or less the same basic kit. In ordinary circumstances, we have the same physical senses as each other; our brains are structured in broadly the same ways and do the same sorts of things, and we have the same internal organs and systems. The fact that you are a human being in the first place and not a bat or a dog means that you came into the world with a basic set of aptitudes that are typical to our species.

If you were a bat or a dog, you'd have to do without many of the aptitudes that you currently take for granted, like articulate language, imagination and opposable thumbs. On the other hand, you'd have other aptitudes that bats and dogs take for granted. Being human, you can't fly without outside help. You're probably not very good at echolocation either or at hanging upside down for months on end. Bats are complacent about such things. Unlike dogs, you're not in demand to follow faint scent trails in the woods or to herd flocks of sheep to the sound of a shrill whistle. Dogs can take these things in their stride.

Because you are human and not something else, certain general aptitudes come as standard issue and some do not. Within these general aptitudes, you have your own personal strengths and weaknesses that are part of your unique biological inheritance. Just as you have your own fingerprints and DNA profile, you have a unique profile of aptitudes, as we all do. This next exercise builds on the last one and is an initial way of helping you to identify the things that come easily to you and those that do not. Remember, aptitudes have to do with your natural strengths and weaknesses. For this exercise, focus just on those. You should think here purely about what you're naturally good at, and not whether you like or dislike doing it. We'll come to your passions and preferences later. This exercise is just about aptitudes.

Exercise Four: What Are You Good At?

- Write your name in the middle of a large piece of paper and draw a circle around it. Look at the categories you developed in Exercise Three. Draw a circle for each of them on the new page so they form a circular pattern around your name with plenty of space between everything. Draw a line from each these circles to the one with your name in it.

- Think of all the things you do in each of these areas and the aptitudes they use. Write some keywords or draw some images for these aptitudes into the relevant circles.
- Think about which of these activities you're naturally good at, which ones you're average at, and which ones you feel you're not so good at. Pick different colors for good, average and not-so-good and highlight each of the items on your map.
- On a new sheet of paper, make three columns, or circles if you prefer. Name them "good," "average" and "not so good." List all the aptitudes you've identified for yourself in the appropriate column or circle.
- You should now have three groups of aptitudes, roughly categorized as good, average and not so good. Take a moment and ask yourself how well this list represents you. Would you move anything around? Would you add or subtract anything? It's your list and it's about you so feel free to play with it until you're happy.
- Look closely at the first group—the areas where you feel you're good. As you look, think of these questions: When and how did you discover that you are good at these things? Do they have anything in common? Are there other ways in which you could apply these aptitudes? What sorts of roles and occupations depend on them?

This exercise is a first attempt at identifying your aptitudes. It depends on your already having some sense of what they are. It's perfectly possible that you have many others that you don't know about. You may have many hidden depths. Concealed within them there may be other important clues to your Element.

Hidden Depths

You may not know what all your aptitudes are because you may never have called on some of them. They lie latent and undiscovered within you. Whether you discover them depends to some extent on opportunity. Music is a good example. Most people have far more musical aptitude than they realize. A powerful example of this possibility is the extraordinary music program in Venezuela known as El Sistema.

In the mid-1970s, Venezuela did not have a single orchestra composed of Venezuelans, and music education was virtually nonexistent. This shouldn't come as a huge surprise. The country as a whole was beset by poverty, crime and political unrest. Support for classical music wasn't just low on the political agenda—it wasn't on the agenda at all. Venezuela seemed to be one of the last places on Earth where something as allegedly "elitist" as classical music could flourish. Yet today, while many of those conditions remain, Venezuela, a nation of only twenty-nine million people, has more than four hundred thousand children intensely involved in learning classical music, and one of the most vibrant orchestral scenes in the world.

This nation, with the ninety-second largest economy in the world and twenty-eight percent of its people living below the poverty line, has produced a growing class of classical musicians in recent decades. Undoubtedly, there were millions of Venezuelans who came of age before the mid-seventies who had the potential to be gifted musical artists but never even picked up an instrument. All of that changed, though, when José Antonio Abreu founded El Sistema.

Abreu is a Venezuelan economist who was also a passionate pianist. Believing that music could be a path for the underprivileged to find community and purpose, he started a program to teach students the skills to perform challenging pieces. He began with just eleven students. "Music and art education were at that time confined to families who could afford to buy instruments," he said. "I felt that music education and art should be part of the patrimony of the whole country."

The first concert of Venezuela's new youth orchestra was on April 30, 1975. Overcoming challenges in funding and a general lack of familiarity with this type of music in the country, the program grew exponentially. It soon became sponsored by the government, and is now being exported to many other nations, including the United States. The program's most celebrated alumnus is Gustavo Dudamel, now Music Director of the Los Angeles Philharmonic and one of the most acclaimed conductors in the world. He was born and raised in Venezuela and has been deeply immersed in the methods and vision of El Sistema. "Our message through music," says Dudamel, "is that everyone has a chance to have a future, together."

There are many remarkable things about El Sistema, including its ability to inspire kids to reach higher and its value in insulating them from the hardships of the outside world—with incidents of gang fighting and police brutality sometimes right outside the door. "This is a radical social project," Charlotte Higgins wrote in an article about El Sistema in *The Guardian*, "in which children, often living in unthinkable circumstances, are given the chance to punch through the poverty cycle—with the help of skills learned through music."

Children start with El Sistema as young as two years old and they understand quickly that they are essential parts of something bigger. El Sistema has a powerful focus on the orchestra as a community that accomplishes much more together than its members ever could alone. The point is not to be the best but to be the best you can be. The height of achievement for these children is to be part of the national youth orchestra. Many of them would never get this perspective otherwise. Without El Sistema they would probably be steeped in the precise opposite message.

Perhaps El Sistema is most notable for bringing out aptitudes in children they otherwise would never have known they had. We don't know how many parents who enroll their children in El Sistema believe that their child will become a professional musician. What we can assume is that they believe that being part of El Sistema helps their children to think differently about themselves and the world around them, and once they begin to do that, they open themselves up to an enormous range of possibilities that they would never have experienced otherwise.

This is true of your own life. If you open yourself to new experiences, the odds improve exponentially of one of those experiences changing your world in a profoundly positive way. Just as those children might never have known they were talented musicians if this program didn't cause them to look in that direction, there may be many things that you are naturally good at if you were only exposed to them. You may have all kinds of aptitudes that you don't know about because the opportunity hasn't arisen to find out. Take cooking.

Jamie Oliver is the award-winning celebrity chef known for his campaigns in the UK and the United States to promote healthy eating and to combat the risks of processed foods and soft drinks. His book *The Naked Chef* was published in 1990 and was just the first in a series of international bestsellers. His television series have been seen in more than forty countries. Yet none of this seemed likely when he was at school. "I was crap at school," he says. "I didn't enjoy work at school at all and I didn't connect with most of it. In a lot of ways I was a problem student. But I seemed to blossom in the kitchen. The lovely thing about cooking is that it can bring out the best in anyone. It is a very hands-on, heartfelt, touchy, smelly, feely, tasty sort of job and you don't have to be an academic genius to do it well."

He was so grateful for his success as a chef that he wanted to offer the same opportunity to others. In 2005, he took out a two-million-dollar loan against his own home to open a nonprofit restaurant to offer work experience to fifteen unemployed young people, some of whom, on their own admission, were virtually unemployable. It was a long and turbulent journey. Some of the trainees were constantly late and uncooperative. "There were times," Oliver says, "when I thought, God, these guys are going to have to work in my kitchen and serve my customers."

Eventually, the restaurant, called, appropriately enough, Fifteen, opened only a little behind schedule and to wide critical acclaim. Ten of the original fifteen trainees met the high standards Oliver set for them and some went on to become professional chefs. The project and the restaurant continue to flourish with fifteen new trainees being recruited every year. If not for this program and Oliver's tireless efforts to promote the start of each new cohort, as he calls each class of apprentices, so that candidates can discover the opportunity for personal growth, these young chefs would be on completely different paths.

"School wasn't great for me as I got into a lot of trouble and never properly learnt the basics such as reading and writing," said Jamie Roberts, a Fifteen apprentice. "After leaving school I worked in a few different jobs but was also in and out of prison. The course at Fifteen caught my eye and I thought it would be a good way to turn my life around and get on the right track."

"To be honest," said Emily Hunt, another apprentice, "I don't know what I'd be doing if it hadn't been for this. Working in a cardboard box factory, probably." Before Emily discovered that she loved cooking, she'd bounced from position to position. "Just a string of crap jobs, really." Oliver's initiative shows that often other people see our aptitudes before we do.

One of the reasons I became so interested in education professionally was because of my own education. When I was in the senior years of high school, some friends and I asked the school if we could put on a play. We used to study play texts in English classes, but we never performed them. One of the teachers agreed to help us put on a play and to direct it as an after-school activity. As this was an all-boys' school, we looked for a play with an all-male cast. There aren't as many of these as you might imagine. We lighted on *Journey's End* by R. C. Sherriff, a classic depiction of life in the trenches in the First World War. I agreed to be stage manager. We loved working on the production, and it was all a great success. The next year we decided to stage *She Stoops to Conquer* by Richard Sheridan. This play has women in it. As we didn't want to perform in drag, we cast around for a solution. Then we had a breakthrough. We would have actual girls in it. Finding girls in an all-boys' school is a challenge. However, across the playing fields, like an exotic parallel universe, there was the all-girls' school.

The two schools collaborated only on two occasions a year. One was the Christmas dance, which was always an awkward and self-conscious affair. The other was the annual health lectures, which were worse. The senior students from both schools combined in our school hall to be given unsettling information on our respective sorts of bodies. There were two lectures, one on smoking and the other on sex. The general theme of both was, "Don't do it. It's bad for your health."

Two of us from our production group asked our head teacher

if we could borrow some girls from the other school to be in the play. He suggested that we talk to the girls' head teacher. We set off across the playing fields like an expeditionary force to an unknown civilization. The girls' head teacher met us cordially but with some curiosity. She thought this was a wonderful idea and agreed immediately to our request. A week later, three real girls arrived for the read-through of the play. The production broke all records for both schools.

Fired by our success, we planned our next production, *The Importance of Being Earnest* by Oscar Wilde. Again, we asked the teacher if he would direct it. He said he couldn't this time but would help us cast it. We all sat around one evening in a large circle and he went through the list of characters, allocating roles. One by one, all the parts went to other members of the group. Resigned to stage-managing again, I sat and waited while he made a final proposal. "I can't direct this production," he said. "I think Ken should do it." I was stunned. It had never crossed my mind that I either could or should direct this or any other play. To my amazement everyone in the group nodded in agreement with him. I did direct the production and found that I was good at it and loved doing it.

It was that experience more than any other that kindled my interest in drama, and that interest became the foundation of my studies in college and my early work in education. If that teacher hadn't seen something in me that I hadn't seen in myself, my life might have gone in a very different direction.

Finding Your Aptitudes

One way to learn more about your own aptitudes—the ones you know about already and the ones you might not—is to take a range of different aptitude tests. There is a huge amount of research into the nature of aptitudes and there are many published and online resources that you can use to explore your own. They include many tests, quizzes and exercises. A few words of caution. Many of these tests are commercial products and some are of questionable scientific value. Some involve registering for newsletters or online employment agencies, but several are truly free. If nothing else, they are entertaining. Occasionally, they're even instructive. It's probably worth your time to have fun with a few of these as a starter simply by typing "aptitude tests" into your search engine.

Beyond this are several tests that have been around for many years and have been administered millions of times. Keep in mind, though, that some aptitude tests can be misleading, if not actually wrong, and you should treat all of them with a questioning attitude. Beware the Forer Effect—believing a generic statement was tailored for you. For example, as part of the research for this book, my son James and I signed up for a practical assessment of our own aptitudes with one of the larger commercial testing organizations. We had two three-hour sessions, which involved timed written tests, multiple-choice questionnaires, manipulating objects, discriminating tones and rhythms, matching sequences of patterns and colors, and tests of memory, arithmetic, vocabulary and time management.

The tests were all interesting in themselves and for the most part they seemed fairly accurate. They showed, for example, that I'm stronger than James in manual dexterity, which I am, and that he has a better musical sense, which he does. In other cases, though, the results were so wide of the mark we wondered if we'd been given the right results. One test ranked him well above average for planning and foresight. He almost didn't get this information because, as usual, he was more than twenty minutes late for the meeting. My color sense and spatial intelligence are apparently so highly developed that the results pointed clearly to a career in interior design. When I mentioned this to my family, the general hysteria went on uninterrupted for almost half an hour.

The problem was not so much in the raw results of the tests as in the interpretation of them, which in this case was done by a computer. As it happens, the whole process failed to identify any of the aptitudes around which my own work for the past forty years has actually revolved, including writing and speaking. They also failed to pinpoint James's natural aptitudes for performance, writing and comedy, at which he excels.

We were told that it's hard to design standardized tests for these things. And therein lies the problem. The limitation these career aids all have is that they are paper-and-pencil tests (or the electronic equivalent) and none of them are likely to tell you that you might be good at playing jazz clarinet. They simply aren't looking for that sort of thing—although that sort of thing might be precisely where you find your Element. At this stage in the technology, if you want to find out more about your aptitudes you're better off taking all such tests with a large pinch of salt. Consider all of these tests critically and ask yourself if they really do apply to you or if you're bending your self toward them because you want to believe them.

There is also a range of tests that you might well have taken already in school or at work, though you might not recognize them by name. Here are four that you may find it interesting to take a look at and compare your results.

The General Aptitude Test Battery (GATB) was created by

the U.S. Department of Labor and has been around for decades. It measures aptitude in nine areas: general learning ability, verbal aptitude, numerical aptitude, spatial aptitude, form perception, clerical perception, motor coordination, finger dexterity and manual dexterity. There are twelve portions to the test overall, though not every portion is administered to everyone. One needs to be GATB-certified to be allowed to administer the test. You can learn more about this test at http://www.careerchoiceguide.com/general-aptitude-test-battery.html.

The Gallup Organization's Clifton StrengthsFinder is an online test that identifies one's "greatest potential for building strengths." It was created by Dr. Donald O. Clifton and a team of scientists from Gallup. The test involves 177 questions and covers a wide range of aptitudes. The test was the foundation for two bestselling books, *Now, Discover Your Strengths* and *StrengthsFinder*. If you want to learn more about StrengthsFinder, you can go to http://strengths.gallup.com/default.aspx.

The Vocational Research Institute's CareerScope test is a combined interest and aptitude test. Through a series of questions, it identifies where your career interests lie and how those match up with your aptitudes. You can find out more about CareerScope at http://www.vri.org/products/careerscope-v10/benefits.

The O*NET Ability Profiler is an assessment created by the Occupational Information Network, creator of the O*NET Database that defines the key features of hundreds of occupations. It tests in nine key areas—verbal ability, arithmetic reasoning, computation, spatial ability, form perception, clerical perception, motor coordination, finger dexterity and manual dexterity (if these categories sound similar to the GATB, this is because the U.S. Department of Labor is involved with both)—and links the findings to

O*NET OnLine, which defines more than eight hundred occupations. For more information about O*NET, go to http://www.onetcenter.org/AP.html.

Assessing Your Path

Since every standardized assessment test I encountered up to the writing of *The Element* seemed to contain some kind of flaw or inconsistency, I broadened my search in the writing of this book for more personalized and sophisticated forms of assessment. One such process has been developed over many years by Dr. Brian Schwartz, a career counselor who is currently Dean of The Institute for Career and Talent Management in Beijing. Dr. Schwartz is the creator of an assessment process he calls SuccessDNA.

While Dr. Schwartz uses the same approach with all of his clients, this assessment program is anything but standardized. "I provide a holistic approach to people that enables them to make career choices based on who they are as human beings," he told me. "People often make decisions based on what they think will make the most money. At the end of the day though, as the Declaration of Independence states, it is the pursuit of happiness that is most important. That requires being authentic, being real. In order for people to be authentic, they have to be self-aware."

Dr. Schwartz's assessment process is as elaborate as any I've seen. If most assessment tests are the equivalent of an off-the-rack suit from a discount store, SuccessDNA is hand-tailored on Savile Row. Interestingly, the first step in the process is a Myers-Briggs-style type-and-temperament test built from Schwartz's own methodology. "I engage my clients in conversations where I give them information about each of the four Myers-Briggs mental functions, using everyday situations to help them get an accurate picture of their type that they validate."

After that comes a series of autobiographical interviews. He starts with questions about a client's grandparents: the nature of their ethnic and religious background, their level of education, what they did for a living, and so forth. He asks similar questions, though not in the same detail, about aunts, uncles and cousins in an effort to get "a social history of sorts of the family."

The reason Dr. Schwartz examines family history so carefully is that he sees family background as fundamental to a person's outlook on career. "I discovered that self-esteem was a critical factor in the career assessment and planning equation. People rise to the level of success that their self-esteem can absorb. Those with low self-esteem don't feel worthy of the rewards that come with success, however they define it. So often, people will talk about their fear of failure and I will find that it's a mask for the fear of success. Underneath it is the feeling that I don't deserve whatever success there might be in life."

Once this part of the autobiography process is over, Dr. Schwartz guides clients through the charting of the highlights of their lives using a method similar to the one developed by Bernard Haldane and popularized by Richard Boles in *What Color Is Your Parachute?* From this, the client picks out the seven experiences, themes or relationships that are most enjoyable or satisfying in their lives. They write brief essays on each and then analyze the experiences to identify the skills they used in these, ultimately identifying which of these skills they most enjoyed. They then pick their ten to fifteen favorite skills, build "skill teams," and compare these teams to each other.

"At this point, the client has a template to put over any job description to see if he or she will be aligned with the work. Of course, in a recession, people don't always hold out for great alignment, but at the end of the day they're really buying a ticket to misery if they don't."

Dr. Schwartz's approach might be more extensive than most people want to—or even can—use, but it is fascinating to see someone employing something so far from the simple questionnaire-and-basic-test models.

How Many Paths Can You Take?

Is it possible to have more than one Element? Of course it is. You have many aptitudes and your Element may evolve over time as your talents mature and your interests change. Personal aptitudes may also move you into a related field. Elizabeth Payne came to designing clothes by a very indirect route. Now Professor of Costume Design at Fresno State, Elizabeth had a strong idea of her Element at a very young age. Interestingly, it came thanks to someone who was still searching for hers.

"My mom went through all these periods when I was a kid," she told me. "She did catering for a couple of years. Then she did painting for a couple of years. Then she did self-help for a couple of years. When I was only four or five, she went through this painting period where she was taking art classes and then ultimately teaching them. I would go with her, and I was always drawing. I thought artists were really cool, and I wanted to be like them. I knew I wanted to be an artist from the time I was a little kid."

Growing up in a tiny village in southern Ohio, Elizabeth didn't find many people other than her mother who encouraged her passion for art. They even convinced her that at best she might become a high school art teacher and maybe do a little painting on the side. Since art was all she ever loved, Elizabeth was okay with this. Then, when she was in high school, her art teacher had a heart attack and was away from school for the rest of the year. The school replaced the teacher with a substitute who was unqualified in art and wasn't even authorized to grade projects. This was not good for someone with Elizabeth's aspirations. Fortunately, an interested English teacher looked at some of Elizabeth's drawings and was so impressed that she entered Elizabeth into an art competition at a local college.

The competition was in costume design, something that Elizabeth knew nothing about. She discovered, though, that her skills in art aligned beautifully with the talents necessary to be a good costume designer. She had an aptitude for it—so much aptitude that she won the competition all four years she entered. Equally important, she loved doing it so much that she decided to study costume design in college and to make it her career if she could.

Having focused on art in high school, she applied to colleges with art departments, only to discover that the costume design programs are usually based in theater departments. Once she mastered that bit of information, she was on her way.

"I knew I could draw very well and that this was an asset. In the program I got into, they made it very clear that I needed to know how to sew and I needed to know how to tell people what I wanted them to make. I worked in a little outdoor theater in North Carolina and sewed on labels and buttons all summer. Then I had a costume designer internship in Massachusetts. I learned all about shopping and sources and how you have to go out to find what you need. I learned about dyeing fabric and creating what you needed when you couldn't get it. My next job was at the Santa Fe Opera. I sewed a lot of buttons that year, too. I also learned a lot about singers and personality types and how to think really quickly if something goes wrong. I'd never had any theater experience before this, so I needed to understand everything that goes on, and what my place in it was."

A college degree led to a graduate degree, and this took her to the Manhattan theater world.

"I worked with a couple of little companies and I learned that I'm not really a for-profit theater person. I don't like working with producers. I got the feeling that the story wasn't important to them; it was mostly about getting a show on Broadway. My feeling was that if the story wasn't good, it didn't matter how much money you threw at costumes or sets. I started looking at nonprofits, which usually means getting involved with schools in some way."

She sent her résumé to various colleges and, because some of her work had been with universities, several of the colleges assumed that she had experience teaching. One offered her a classroom position and, as she said, "I just went with it." Elizabeth then found out she was good at something she hadn't considered before. She was a born teacher. Her ability as a teacher came from a natural aptitude for helping people learn combined with her professional expertise in her field. "When I entered costume design, I didn't think I'd ever be able to teach anybody, and I feel like because of the professional experiences I've had, I'm a good teacher. I'm not just teaching theory. I'm teaching them what it's like to be out there."

Elizabeth Payne discovered some of her aptitudes when she was very young. She went on to discover others that she hadn't even suspected she had.

Seeing Differently

You may also find that the road you're on becomes blocked and you have to explore other options. If you do that properly, you'll find you have more aptitudes than you thought and more ways forward in your life than you think.

In many ways, Noppadol Bunleelakun got a raw deal at the start of his life. For one thing, it started too soon. He was born two months early and weighed less than three pounds at birth. To save his life, doctors kept him in an incubator and gave him extra oxygen. The procedure allowed him to live, but it also destroyed his optic nerves and made him irreversibly blind. Noppadol went to a school for the blind in his native Bangkok, where they taught him the things they taught all students like him: Braille, working with his hands, basic academics. One day when he was six, Noppadol heard another student playing piano, and he gravitated toward the sound that was unlike any other he'd ever heard. "The piano became my friend," he told a reporter for the *Bangkok Post*. "I spent most of my free time with it."

A teacher helped him learn the instrument, holding Noppadol's hands over the keyboard and pressing the correct notes down with him. The learning process was slow and often frustrating. However, by the time he was eleven Noppadol didn't need anyone else's hands to help him play the instrument. In fact, he needed nothing at all, other than to hear a piece of music a few times, to be able to replicate it.

At that point, Noppadol needed to put his music education aside. His family couldn't afford private lessons, and his new school focused exclusively on academics. For five years, he played the piano much less—he didn't have one at home—so he could keep up in his classes with sighted students. Then a teacher discovered his talent, agreed to give him lessons for free, and Noppadol was on a path to truly making the most of his capacities. At age twenty-one, he released two jazz albums simultaneously on a major Thai label, and then two more the next year. It would be an extraordinary output for any musician; for one who had to cross so many hurdles simply to play an instrument, it was nothing short of miraculous.

These days, Noppadol is known best by two nicknames: Joe the Pianist and Mobile Karaoke. The former was obviously invented by those who preferred not to attempt to wrap their tongues around his given name. The latter is a reference to his remarkable ability to play nearly anything after hearing it only a few times. A career as a jazz pianist wasn't what anyone had in mind for Noppadol Bunleelakun when he started his studies at Bangkok School for the Blind, but his desire to go beyond the limitations of visual impairment drove him to develop capacities no one guessed he might have.

Few of us need to deal with as many obstacles to get to our passions as Noppadol did. Yet we sometimes face a different kind of blindness. We don't see what we're capable of because we don't see our own possibilities. You may assume falsely that certain paths are closed to you or you may not know where to look for them. Either way, you may be missing ways to be in your Element.

There is another dimension to discovering your aptitudes. You may believe that you don't have an aptitude for something— math, or music, or design, or whatever it may be—because you originally encountered it in the wrong way, or because you were taught it in school in a way that conflicted with how you really learn. To understand more fully what your aptitudes are, you need to think about your own preferred ways of thinking and about your own learning styles. These are the focus of the next chapter. Before we move on, though, here are some questions to consider based on what we've discussed so far in this chapter:

- What sorts of activities come especially easily to you?
- What do you feel your natural talents are?

- How did you first become aware of them?
- Do you have any aptitudes that you've never considered developing?
- Do you have any talents that you haven't developed but wished that you had?
- Do you have any talents that you've been discouraged from developing?
- If you've ever taken any aptitude tests, did any of the results surprise you?
- Which of your aptitudes do you think you could really develop if you tried?

CHAPTER THREE

How Do You Know?

DEVELOPING YOUR APTITUDES assumes that you know what they are in the first place. As we saw in the last chapter, for a number of reasons, it's possible that you do not. This chapter explains in more detail why you may be having trouble with knowing what you're good at and offers you some help with finding out. Before we move on, though, let's continue to take stock of where you are at the moment. Try this exercise. It will give you some personal reference points for the themes we're about to consider.

Exercise Five: How Do You Know?

In Exercise Four you made three lists: things at which you're good, average and not so good. Look now at the second two columns or circles: the things at which you feel average or not so good. Think about them in relation to these questions.

- Do they have anything in common?
- What makes you think you're average or not so good at these things?

- What have been your experiences of doing them?
- Have you ever been encouraged to practice them properly? What happened?
- Do you wish you were better at them or are you not interested?
- Are you interested in revisiting them and trying a different approach?

As before, you might find it helpful to do some automatic writing around these questions, or to sketch some thoughts, or create a collage of images that express your experience of these activities and your feelings about them.

For reasons that we're coming to, it may well be that you have more aptitude—and more flair—for some activities that you've already tried than you realize. Your average or poor assessment of yourself may be because you encountered them in the wrong way. We'll come back to this possibility later in the chapter.

There's another reason why you may not know what you're good at. Opportunity. The lists you've made so far are of things that you've already experienced. What about the things you've never tried? How would you know whether you're good at something if you've had no experience of it? As I said earlier, the Element doesn't come with a quota. You may have several, including some of which you're unaware simply through lack of opportunity. It's perfectly possible that you might be very good at various things you've never attempted or even know about.

If you live far from the ocean and have never set foot in a boat, how would you know if you have any aptitude for sailing? If you've never been on horseback, how would you know how well you might ride? What if you've never picked up a violin or a trumpet, or held a pool cue, or tried carpentry or weaving, or been in a laboratory, or played chess, or tried to cook, or cultivate a garden, or work with children or speak French? How would you know?

You may have all kinds of latent talents that lie undiscovered beneath the surface, like minerals in the ground. Part of finding your Element is being open to the possibility that it might lie in a field you've never explored. If you're casting about for what you should do with your life, limiting your horizons can have dramatic consequences.

That was certainly what was going on with Sam, a Malaysian teen. Her parents exposed her to a number of activities, including violin, ballet, art and swimming. All of these were activities that Sam had shown some interest in, but the structure and the pressure she felt from organized programs in these areas caused her systematically to drop each of them. As she did so, she became withdrawn, irritable and restless, and had trouble making friends.

Then Sam saw a street dancing competition on television called *Showdown*. She found an instant connection to this form of dance and told her mother that this was what she wanted to do. Her mother tried to find a place where Sam could learn this wildly energetic, highly acrobatic form of dance, but couldn't come up with anything. Sam, however, was relentless, believing that she'd found something that she loved that she could be very good at. Eventually, the two of them found the academy that pioneered street dance training in Malaysia, and Sam enrolled.

"From then on," her mother said in a blog post, "she has been dancing every night at the school, joining every class she could possibly get herself in, and learning all the different dances offered there—from whacking to locking to reggae to house to girl-style to hip hop . . . You name it, she can dance it! She was probably the most diligent student there, as she could never get enough of dancing!"

Sam went from sullen to driven, regularly saying that she was doing what she wanted to do for the rest of her life. Not only was this something she cared about passionately, it was also something she was very, very good at. This became clear all over Malaysia when Sam and her dance group "The Hype" appeared in the 2012 season of *Showdown* and made it into the top twelve.

Sam has found something for which she has an extremely high level of aptitude, and in doing so she is exponentially happier and now has a strong sense of purpose. It all began because she was exposed to something of which she'd previously been completely unaware, that genuinely clicked for her.

You Can't Be Serious

Finding your Element depends on having the opportunities to discover what you're really capable of. One vital strategy is to do all you can to create those opportunities and to explore new avenues of possibility in yourself and in the world around you. In practice, of course, doing this may not be so simple. In some circumstances, some avenues for self-discovery may be discouraged or restricted.

One reason you may not know some of your aptitudes may be the culture you live in. Biology affects the aptitudes that you're born with; culture can seriously affect whether you discover and develop them. All cultures smile or frown upon different particular activities and lifestyles. What's accepted in one may be beyond the pale in another. Finding your Element may bring you up against these conventions.

The culture you live in may inhibit and possibly prohibit you from certain paths according to your age, gender, sexuality and ethnicity and what, exactly, it is that you want to do. Cultural constraints can range from raised eyebrows over dinner to solitary confinement without parole. In Matthew Lee's case, they were noncustodial but socially deterring nonetheless.

Like most people, Matthew Lee is good at many things. He is a good web designer, and he has made a fine living from it. However, there is one thing that he is really good at and loves doing so much that he gets lost in it. Matthew Lee is a magician. "I had been fascinated with magic since I was eight," he told me. "I first saw a magician perform on a cruise liner. He had this cloth and he made it turn into a cane in less than a second. I was eight and it left a deep impression on me."

The impression only went so far. "I didn't think about it much after that. I went through school, I studied, I became a computer engineer. Then I was walking in a mall and I saw a magic shop. It was the day after I graduated college. I remembered that incident from when I was a kid and I thought, let's see what happens." Matthew spent some time in the store, and on a whim he bought some magic paraphernalia. He already had his career mapped out, and had never considered magic as a profession because in Singapore, where he lived, no one took magicians seriously or gave them any real respect at all. Still, he took his new toys home and began to practice, just to entertain himself.

"I found when I practiced that I began to lose all sense of time. I'd practice in front of a mirror for hours trying to get something right, making sure it looked correct from that one angle. I just did it over and over again. It can be very Zen— suddenly you look out the window and it's morning. I didn't feel tired; I just wanted to get this thing right. That's how I got into it. I guess you like it because you realize you're good at it. It's kind of a chicken or egg sort of thing. You like it because you're good at something. I was never good at that level at anything before that."

It was a revelation for Matthew to discover that he was multi-talented. He'd done well in school. Directly out of college, he found a job doing web design for an agency, and his clients were very happy with his work. But he knew inside that he wasn't allowing his greatest talent to emerge. He was keeping his most accomplished skill between himself and his mirror. As his fascination with magic grew, Matthew started to think about what it might be like to perform in public.

"There's the Singapore Magic Circle Forum online. People were always saying the same thing—if you want to explore how this is going to work, you have to volunteer for charity events and see how things go. That's what I did. I volunteered for an event for the Children's Cancer Foundation. There were a whole bunch of magicians there and it was my first time performing. I got there and I did my thing. For some reason, the nervousness I felt before I went on just went away. There were other magicians there and they asked me how long I'd been in magic. They were thinking I'd been around for two or three years, but it had only been six months."

Matthew had more talent than he knew and enough passion for magic that he began to wonder if it could be more than a hobby. That's when circumstance came into play. He had a web design client who happened to produce magic shows all over Singapore. Matthew soon had someone booking his act. Within a relatively short span, he went from entertaining his own reflection to dazzling crowds. Soon he was making enough money as a magician to become a freelance web designer, which allowed him to do more magic gigs and spend more time mastering his craft.

The professional transition was seamless, especially because he was making more money and in less time as a freelancer than he had been as a salaried employee. The personal transition was less so. "My wife had a fit when she first learned I was going to do magic productions because she thought it would be unstable. She eventually came around when she realized how happy I am."

He's still dealing with the stigma attached to his profession in Singapore. The fact that he's a magician isn't usually the first thing he brings up when he meets someone, or, for that matter with those he's known for a very long time. His parents, for example, only recently learned that he does this professionally. For now, he's more concerned with refining his talents than with toppling cultural conventions. And he does spend a great deal of time refining his talents. He often stays up until two or three in the morning working on his illusions and learning from the best role models he can find. "I wouldn't say I'm extremely good at it. That's Penn and Teller. I'm at a level where I'm good enough to perform for money. I got there and I didn't feel as if I put in any work until I thought about all the practicing I'd done. But that was play to me."

Matthew Lee's version of play allows him to build upon a natural aptitude that he might have never discovered if he hadn't seen that cruise ship performer and if he hadn't taken a momentary detour from his planned career path to stop by a little shop in a mall. He always had it in him to be a magician. However, if not for circumstance and his determination to swim against the cultural tide, this aptitude—and the burning passion that accompanies it—might never have surfaced.

The Perils of Education

You may be hampered in your quest for your Element by the general conventions of your culture. But most cultures also have a systematic process of conditioning, which is especially significant for finding—or not finding—your natural aptitudes. Ironically, it is the very process that you'd imagine would help you to discover them. I mean education.

The Element has a lot to say about education and so does my book *Out of Our Minds: Learning to Be Creative.* If you have a particular interest in these issues, you can do no better than to download them both immediately. For our purposes here, there are two ways in which formal education often gets in the way of finding your Element. The first is that most systems of education operate on a very narrow view of aptitudes. The second is that they often disregard the different ways in which individuals actually learn.

More Than You Think

What do students mainly do at school? For the most part, they sit at desks, reading, writing, calculating and doing low-grade clerical work. Why is this? One of the primary reasons is that schools mainly emphasize certain sorts of academic aptitude, including particular forms of verbal and mathematical reasoning. Often too they equate intelligence in general with the much narrower idea of IQ. These sorts of aptitudes are very important, but there is much more to your aptitudes than can be revealed in conventional academic work or IQ tests.

One of the consequences of this preoccupation is that schools typically give low status to so-called nonacademic work, including the visual and performing arts, physical education, and practical and "vocational" programs. The result is that very many students, even those who are good at academic work, never discover the real range of their aptitudes, especially if they lie in these other, neglected areas.

All the time that my brother Derek was developing his expertise in engineering, he was generally distracted, bored and often in trouble at school. None of the things that he was actually good at seemed to count in school and weren't taken into account in reports and assessments. Apart from his engineering talents, he taught himself to play a whole range of musical instruments, including keyboards and the ukulele. He was so good that he regularly played in our local church from the age of ten, and as an adult he worked as a professional musician in clubs and theaters across the region. Despite his obvious and abundant talents, he continued to do badly in school. This is true of very many people who have a feel for making things and working with their hands as well as their minds.

By the way, because they have such a narrow view of ability, school systems usually promote a very wide idea of disability. For six years, from when I was five until I was eleven, I went to a school for the "physically handicapped." They weren't quite as good at euphemisms then as they are now. I was surrounded by kids with all kinds of physical disabilities—polio, cerebral palsy, hydrocephalus, asthma, epilepsy and lots of others things. We weren't remotely interested in each other's "handicaps." We made friends on the basis of people's interests, attitudes and personalities. They were what mattered. The people I liked were funny, insightful and sensitive, just like other children, disabled or otherwise.

Outside of school, though, we were often defined by our disabilities. We were "handicapped"—a bit like a species. Often when people have a disability, it's the disability that other people see rather than all the other abilities that coexist with their particular difficulty. It's why we talk about people being "disabled" rather than "having a disability." One of the reasons that people are branded by their disability is that the dominant conception of ability is so narrow. But the limitations of this conception affect everyone in education, not just those with "special needs." These days, anyone whose real strengths lie outside the restricted field of academic work can find being at school a dispiriting experience and emerge from it wondering if they have any significant aptitudes at all.

What's Your Style?

The narrow view of ability is one problem in conventional education. A second is the common failure to engage with students' individual learning styles. I said earlier that one of the reasons you feel you have little aptitude for something might be the way in which you first encountered it, and especially if you didn't do well at it in school.

Any conversation among adults about their school days is likely to prompt a series of anecdotes of failure. "I was never any good at science." "I was a terrible writer." "I couldn't even draw stick figures in art class." You've probably shared some of these stories yourself. Of course, you might well be awful at any number of things. You might be genuinely bad at math, for instance. There's nothing wrong with that. I've made peace with it. But you may think you have no aptitude for something because you weren't taught it in a way that connected with how you actually think and learn.

We all learn best in different ways, and your own learning style can strongly affect what you think your aptitudes are. Some schools teach all sorts of disciplines through verbal presentation and written exercises and tests. They don't teach chemistry for visual learners, for example, or calculus for kinesthetic learners. Teaching and learning mainly through words can work well for students who prefer to learn that way. The fact is that many do not. The result is that students can fail to engage with many disciplines and processes that they might otherwise enjoy and excel in.

For most of her time at school, our daughter, Kate, thought she wasn't good at chemistry. Then she had a new chemistry teacher, who changed everything. This is Kate's account of the difference:

"I was not the best student growing up. Well, that's not entirely true. What I should say is that past a certain point, I lost interest. There was a period when I was a great student. I loved reading and writing, art, dance, choir, science and gym. I did not even mind the elaborate British school uniforms. From an early age, I was put in the bottom group for math. At my school, students were organized by color—Blue was the top group, Green the middle, and Green Two the bottom. It seems like a ridiculous system to me now, and the result of constantly being in Green Two for math was that I grew up with a fear of numbers and passionate aversion to anything that involved them. I had a hard time with my multiplication tables, fractions still terrify me, and I have always had a problem dialing phone numbers. Being put in Green Two for math from a young age knocked my confidence. After a while I just took it for granted that I was bad at math, so I never really tried. After all, I got top marks in English and art, French as well, and four days a week I went to ballet class where I could not have been happier. To be honest, math was not my top priority.

"This assumption that I was not good at math followed me to

Los Angeles. Once again, I was placed in the bottom group (Math 3 as it was called) and this time did not even feign attention. I rarely turned in my homework, and spent the majority of the classes doodling. If I didn't try and I failed, it was because I hadn't tried, not because I wasn't smart. It was a powerful excuse, and I hid behind it for years. Surprisingly, my math teachers didn't seem to mind and all gave me passing grades. Soon enough, I found myself out of middle school and sitting in a tenth grade chemistry class.

"I had always liked science, and up until chemistry it had included little to no mathematical technique. I liked science mostly because it meant drawing lots of pictures of the evaporation cycle or making things such as a boat that could float in a tank of water. Chemistry, with its endless numbers on the table of elements and fraction-like equations, did not. In fact, it terrified me. I failed out of chemistry after the first semester midterms. For the rest of tenth grade I had an extra free period, which I thought was brilliant. Problem solved. Until eleventh grade, when I found myself enrolled back in tenth grade chemistry.

"My new teacher, Ms. Miller, walked in and began the class. I spent the entire fifty minutes passing notes to my friend at the desk next to me. This went on until the first test, which of course I failed. No problem, I thought, but Ms. Miller was not impressed. Unlike all of the previous teachers, Ms. Miller did not just pass it off as one failing student in a class of otherwise straight A's. She called me into her office, told me off for choosing to sit at the back of the class, not paying attention and not completing the homework assignments. She said that my behavior and attitude were unacceptable for a person of my capabilities. I was embarrassed and ashamed. She didn't stop there, though. She said that if I agreed to her conditions she would tutor me during my free periods and lunch. Her conditions were that I move to the front of the class and that I commit to putting work into chemistry. What could I do? I agreed.

"We started the next week. Every day, I would go to Ms. Miller to review that day's class or plan for the one ahead. The progress was instant. I found, miraculously, that as soon as I paid attention (and in one-on-one settings, I had no choice but to do so) I understood the chemistry. Even more surprisingly to me, I loved it. I loved it to the point that I not only got straight A's in chemistry for the rest of the year, and ended up tutoring other students in my class, but I actually considered studying chemistry in college. I looked forward to my chemistry classes and to my chemistry homework. My lab book was filled beautifully. My equations were flawless. I was not even afraid of the numbers.

"I was hooked on chemistry, and all because one teacher recognized a student who was doing well in most of her other classes but was blatantly slacking off in hers. All because of a teacher who saw that I did not thrive in a traditional classroom setup and was so dedicated that she took the time to repeat each lesson plan with me in private.

"She refused to give up on me and refused to let me give up on myself. The benefit was not just seen in my grade point average; my confidence went through the roof. But for Ms. Miller I would have gone through life believing that I was bad at chemistry; that I simply could not do it. She taught me much more than chemistry. She taught me that when I genuinely try at something I can do it. It is a lesson that has affected every aspect of my life."

So, what is your learning style? Well, there are various ways to think about this. While there is abundant evidence that people have a wide range of learning styles, experts differ on the precise definition. The educational theorist David Kolb, for example, believes that one can learn by being a converger (one who is strong in the practical application of ideas, approaches learning in an unemotional fashion, and has relatively narrow interests), a diverger (one who has a strong imagination, is good at generating ideas and seeing things from different perspectives, and has a broad range of interests), an assimilator (one with a strong ability to create theoretical models, who excels in inductive reasoning, and tends to be more concerned with abstract concepts than with people), or an accommodator (one whose greatest strength is doing things, is comfortable taking risks, performs well when required to react to immediate circumstances, and solves problems intuitively).

Richard Felder is co-developer of the Index of Learning Styles. He suggests that there are eight different learning styles. *Active* learners absorb material best by applying it in some fashion or explaining it to others. *Reflective* learners prefer to consider the material before doing anything with it. *Sensing* learners like learning facts and tend to be good with details. *Intuitive* learners like to identify the relationships between things and are comfortable with abstract concepts. *Visual* learners remember best what they see, while *verbal* learners do better with written and spoken explanations. *Sequential* learners like to learn by following a process from one logical step to the next, while *global* learners tend to make cognitive leaps, continuously taking in information until they "get it."

VARK is a guide to learning styles built around a short questionnaire developed by Neil Fleming. It categorizes participants by four learning preferences: *visual* (receiving information from charts, diagrams, maps, etc.), *aural/auditory* (getting information from lectures, recorded presentations, discussions, etc.), *read/*

write (getting information from text, including books, the Internet, PowerPoint presentations, and the like), and *kinesthetic* (getting information through concrete personal experiences).

You can take the VARK questionnaire very quickly at http://www.vark-learn.com/english/page.asp?p=questionnaire. This or another diagnostic of learning style might reveal a preference you didn't know you had. Armed with this preference, you might just want to try to expand the range of what you're good at.

While Kolb, Felder and Fleming offer three different models (and there are many others), they tend to agree on two things. One is that few people, if any, learn the same way all the time; each of us uses all of these styles to some degree as we learn. The other is that most people tend to start somewhere. While we might learn using an amalgam of visual, auditory, reading and kinesthetic processes, the experience of learning tends to be strongest for us when it activates the learning style with which we are most comfortable. If you tend to learn best visually, your mind might tend to wander during a lecture until the professor starts drawing on the whiteboard.

For different students, one teacher may lecture too much, another may rely too heavily on images. Never had much interest in history? Maybe that's because your primary learning style is visual and no one ever helped you to "see" the past as effectively as they could have. Do you have little patience for projects that involve using your hands? Maybe you have a read/write learning orientation and you've never considered studying the process behind a manual exercise before embarking on it.

Many of us wish we were good at poetry or graphic design or mixology or any of a million other things, but have avoided them because our only experiences at trying to learn them were negative. The salesperson that sold you the camcorder attempted to talk you through using it when what you really needed to do was get your hands on the machine. The friend who tried to show you how to knit jumped right to using the needles without ever explaining the underlying concept. If these experiences failed to engage your preferred learning style, there's a strong chance that you absorbed only a fraction of them.

A friend was telling me recently about his daughter's experience with a statistics class in college. She'd been so scarred by her experiences with math in middle school that she'd put off fulfilling her university math requirement until her senior year. She entered the class the first day dreading it and convinced that she was going to dread every minute of it that followed for the entire semester. However, her statistics professor didn't bombard her with equations and theorems. Instead, he told stories that gave practical application to a variety of situations in which statistics came into play. The young woman, who Richard Felder would probably say had a preference for *intuitive* learning, saw connections between the stories and the mathematical work required to make sense of these stories. For the first time since her elementary school days, the woman "got" the concept behind a mathematical process. None of this made her want to turn her back on a career in journalism to get a PhD in serendipitous numerical patterns, but it did help her survive and even thrive in the class.

The key to making the most of your capacities is celebrating how you learn and using that learning style to explore as many interests as possible. Once you accept that how you know things is a critical component of what you know, you're free to apply this to as many disciplines as suits your fancy.

Pay Attention

The failure to engage with individual learning styles can have serious consequences for children in school. One example is the alleged epidemic of attention deficit hyperactivity disorder (ADHD). Don't mistake me. I have never said that there is no such thing as ADD or ADHD. There is broad agreement among healthcare professionals that there is such a condition. What I do question is the rate of diagnosis. Parents report that almost 10 percent or 5.4 million children four to seventeen years of age have been diagnosed with ADHD, as of 2007. The percentage of children with a parent-reported ADHD diagnosis increased by 22 percent between 2003 and 2007. Rates of ADHD diagnosis increased an average of 3 percent per year from 1997 to 2006 and an average of 5.5 percent per year from 2003 to 2007. This is all very good news for the drug companies. According to IMS Health, a drug information company, doctors in the United States wrote 51.5 million prescriptions for ADHD drugs in 2010, with a total sales value of $7.42 billion—an increase of 83 percent from the $4.05 billion sold in 2006.

Are there genuine reasons for an increased incidence of ADHD? Possibly. Diet may be a factor and in particular the massive consumption of processed foods and sugared drinks. Another factor may be the compulsive attractions of digital culture. Spending hours in front of screens can encourage rapid shifts of attention and continuous multitasking. These two factors may account for some of the increased diagnoses of ADHD. Two others certainly do.

Now that ADD and ADHD are such widely publicized conditions, the moment a child looks bored or distracted, someone is likely to reach for a prescription pad. Some cases may be genuine; many may not. Several studies have suggested that in many cases

ADD and ADHD are being diagnosed after the briefest of examinations.

Also, many children are bored and restless in school not because they have a condition but because they are children and what they are required to do is actually boring. I think it was the American actress and comedian Phyllis Diller who said that we spend the first three years of a child's life teaching them to walk and to speak and the next twelve years at school telling them to sit down and shut up. We shouldn't be surprised if many of them find it difficult. Young children have great physical energy and a deep curiosity for the world around them.

I often ask parents whose children have been diagnosed with ADHD if they always have trouble concentrating. Often they don't. When they're doing something that they love, they'll focus for hours and hardly look up. It might be anything from writing music or poetry to working with animals or doing experiments. They don't show signs of ADHD when they are in their Element. If parents, teachers and others adopted and acted on a broader conception of intelligence and learning styles, I have no doubt that many alleged cases of ADHD would disappear.

Becoming Yourself

Resisting the stereotypes of intelligence in education and discovering your latent talents can change the course of your life in profound ways. Hans Zimmer is the Academy and Grammy Award-winning composer of more than a hundred film scores, including those for *The Lion King*, *The Dark Knight*, *Gladiator* and *Inception*. Growing up in Germany and then England, he was a problem pupil for every school he attended. He went to five of them in turn and was eventually "thrown out," as he puts it, of all of them. He was generally restless, bored, disruptive in class, inattentive and miserable with the whole process. He has no doubt that he would have been medicated for ADHD if the diagnosis and drugs had been available at the time. As it was, the only activity that consistently held his attention was music—not in school, but at home, where he was surrounded by music and constantly sat at the piano making up his own tunes.

He left school as soon as he could and tried to make his way as a rock musician. He joined one band after another and eventually had his first commercial success in the 1970s with a band called the Buggles, which recorded the hit song, "Video Killed the Radio Star."

At that time, composing for film wasn't even a distant thought for Hans, not least because he couldn't, and still can't, read conventional music notation. The great turning point in his life came when someone asked for his help with using a Moog sound synthesizer. For him, it was a revelation. He found that he had an intuitive feel for this new way of generating sounds and became fascinated by its potential. Work followed making soundtracks for commercials and small independent movies, and eventually he moved to Hollywood. He has gone on to become one of the world's leading composers for feature films and is in constant demand from directors around the world for his passionate, powerful and deeply sensitive scores.

Hans' studio in Santa Monica is a wonderful mix of high technology and old-fashioned study, somewhere between NASA Mission Control and the library of an old country house. As we sat in front of the large HD movie screen and the banks of computers at which he composes, he explained that he still doesn't read music in the conventional sense. "But if you shove me in front of a computer with a computer musical language I can probably sight-read that for you. I suppose we all find our way of putting systems into place that serve us. If it means reinventing the wheel a couple of times, you do that. The other thing about what I do, and I think it's the most important thing because it's in the description, is that I play."

Zimmer started playing piano at a very young age and he started composing nearly as soon, so not being able to read music was never really an impediment. Perhaps it was even an advantage. For one thing, it led him to look at music in a way that few teachers ever could have taught him. Zimmer learned from the masters, but not the legendary classical composers. Instead, he found inspiration from the great architects.

"I have a really good instinct for patterns and shapes and architecture. The things I write about and find inspiring are the works of architects like Norman Foster and Frank Gehry. I love looking at their buildings and seeing how they've put things together. And very often, when I look at my pieces of music—not in musical notation, obviously, but in the computer—I look at the shape, and when the shape and the patterns look right, they usually sound right. I love what Norman Foster did with the Reichstag in Berlin. He took an appallingly ugly old German building, which had so much bad history. And then he put this amazing modern thing on top of it. The way he managed to combine and merge the old with the new, that's constantly how I see my music. I mean, I'm constantly in some sort of a classical German vocabulary shoving modern technology, shoving rock n' roll and electronics at it.

"It's a funny thing, because people will say, 'Who were the composers that influenced you?' and I can point at all of them. But I can also point at many architects. They haven't influenced me but they have inspired me. At the end of the day, what you really want is the guy who inspires you, not the guy who influenced you."

For Hans Zimmer, music was not only a passion: it was a

pathway to a life of meaning and achievement. To find his path he had to overcome many stereotypes—including ideas about intelligence and achievement in education and about standard techniques of musicianship and composition in his chosen field. Music was very important in his household, and he obviously had a predilection toward it, but his unique achievements have come through following the call of his own talents and being willing to explore the many other fields of creative work through which they have led him.

Expect the Unexpected

To find your Element you may have to challenge your own beliefs about yourself. Whatever age you are, you've almost certainly developed an inner story about what you can do and what you can't do; what you're good at and what you're not good at. You may be right, of course. But for all the reasons we've discussed, you may be misleading yourself. Part of making sense of where you are now is to understand how you got here. So if you do doubt your aptitudes in certain areas, think about how these doubts were first formed. Are there other ways of developing them that you'd enjoy more and surprise yourself in the process? And what about all the aptitudes you may never have used? How can you discover more of those? As the next step in your quest, try this exercise.

Exercise Six: Branching Out

- Make a collage or list of aptitudes you see in other people that you have no idea whether you have or not.
- Highlight the ones you'd be interested to explore in yourself and develop if you could.

- Make a collage or list of activities that you think would draw on these aptitudes.
- Circle the ones you'd be willing to try.
- Make a list of the practical steps you could take to try each of them.

Before you move to the next chapter, here are some more questions for you to reflect on.

- How do you think and learn best?
- Has anyone ever suggested that you might be good at something that you hadn't considered?
- Have you ever avoided doing something because you thought you wouldn't be good at it?
- Have you tried learning something you're "not good at" in a new way?
- Is there anything you feel you might be good at if you had the chance to work at it properly?

CHAPTER FOUR

What Do You Love?

IF YOU'VE BEEN doing the exercises so far and reflecting on the questions, you may have begun to have a clearer idea about your natural strengths and weaknesses—your aptitudes. But being in your Element is not only about doing something you're good at. Many people do things they are good at but don't care for. To be in your Element, you have to love it. So what are passions? Why does it matter that you find yours? And how do you do that?

Many of the people I've spoken with about the Element say that they have a bit of problem with the idea of passion. For some, it's because the word may suggest flashing eyes and pounding hearts and they wonder if they're capable of that and how long they could keep it up. For others, it raises a whole series of other questions. These are some of them:

- What if I have no passions?
- What if I love something I'm not good at?
- What if what I love is morally dubious?
- Who's going to clean the toilets and do the nasty jobs?
- How will I know when I've found my Element?

Towards the end of this chapter, I'll answer each of these questions. To do that, I need first to say what I mean by passion, how it relates to other ideas like love and spirit and what it really means in relation to the Element.

But before we get to that, think first about yourself and the things you love to do—or not. Try this exercise, which builds on your thoughts about your aptitudes.

Exercise Seven: What Do You Enjoy?

- Look again at the list you made in Exercise Four of the things that you're good at. Look through the list of activities you made to which these aptitudes can be applied. Add or change the list if you'd like to in the light of Exercise Five and any other thoughts you've had since.
- Ask yourself: which of the things that you're good at, which:

  a) you really enjoy,
  b) you don't mind doing,
  c) you don't enjoy.

- As before, take a different color for each of these three feelings and highlight each of the things you're good at according to your feelings about them.
- On a separate sheet of paper, make three columns or large circles and list the things you're good at according to these feelings.

Keep this sheet of paper nearby. We'll come back to this exercise and develop it later in the chapter. For now, let's get into the idea of passion through another story.

Feeling Passionate

Most people would hesitate to give a hammer to a four-year-old. The risks range from environmental to dental. When Emily Cummins' grandfather gave her a hammer nothing calamitous happened—but it did fire her passions.

"I used to spend just hours with my granddad in the shed in the bottom of his garden," she told me. "I was absolutely fascinated by his inventiveness and how he could take leftover materials and scraps and create toys for me and my cousins. When I got older, he started to teach me. We started by hammering nails into a workbench, and by the time I was in secondary school, I knew how to use a lathe and create my own toys. There's something so fascinating for me in taking leftover materials and having the excitement of not only building something, but playing with it and feeling rewarded for having created it."

Emily knew instantly that she'd found her passion, though as a preschooler, she probably didn't think of it in those terms. She'd felt a "buzz" right away, and found that nothing else fascinated her anywhere near as much. "My granddad ignited a creative spark in me, which I hope I'll never lose. He allowed me to do things that not all kids could do. He let me experiment with taking things apart and putting them back together. He'd give me little challenges and I was very creative at different ways of making things. When my granddad saw my interest, he was even more enthusiastic in guiding me and allowed me to do more and more. He trusted me to use his machinery and he taught me so well. I made mistakes—I grated my finger on the disc sander—but I can't explain the excitement I had. If my granddad hadn't encouraged me, I wouldn't have known what technology was, because it wasn't taught in school."

By the time Emily got to high school, she'd started entering technology competitions. She'd also refined her purpose. Where once building and inventing was a way of making toys for herself and her cousin, now she wanted to make things that could address real-world problems. For her first major competition, she considered the trouble her other grandfather had getting toothpaste out of a tube because of his arthritis. She built an automatic dispenser for him. "I ended up being judged by some industry experts. I was terrified, because I never liked to speak out. I did the presentation and the judges started criticizing me, and I found a voice that I didn't know I had. I really believed in my product and was passionate about it, and this self-belief came out. I ended up winning because they said they saw that the real passion I had for my product was different from what a lot of the other schoolchildren were doing, which was a PlayStation rack or something along those lines."

For her last competition before going to university, she went for broke. "I decided to take the ridiculous challenge of creating a refrigerator that didn't use any electricity. My teacher was really worried because she knew that this was my last step before university. She said, 'If you mess this one up, you're going to be in trouble.' For me that was the challenge right there.

"I put everything into it. I was meeting with companies. I was doing research. I knew I could do it. I came up with a really simple refrigerator based on evaporation, which, you know, has been around for a number of years—I never claimed to have invented evaporation! It involves heat transfer. You get a completely dry compartment which is hygienic, and you can actually use dirty water to cool the product in the fridge."

The project was a huge success, but Emily's teacher was at least partially right about this affecting her future at university.

While schools would have been glad to have her, she found that she didn't feel the same about them. "My heart wasn't in it at all," she said. Instead, she took a deferment from university and then broke the news to her parents that she was going to go to Africa with her most sophisticated invention.

"I wrote a business plan. I'd never written a business plan before, so I went to my business teacher and came up with a really simple plan. I wound up winning five thousand pounds based on my passion and determination that my product was going to be a success. I did some volunteering work because I was only eighteen at the time and that was the deal I made with my parents. I went to Namibia and worked with a guy who runs a hostel. He took me into a township in Namibia in Wintuk where I tested my fridge. I didn't tell my parents, because they would have been terrified. I started to teach people how to make my fridges. I was using local resources and local materials and I started to create some businesses with these women and they passed along the idea. Now my fridge is used across Namibia, South Africa, Zimbabwe and Botswana."

Emily Cummins embraced her passion at a very young age and continues to build on that passion in profound ways. What do Emily's story and all the others in this book tell us about the nature of passion, particularly as it relates to the Element?

What Is Passion?

The English word "passion" has an interesting history. It comes from the ancient Greek word *paskho*, and its original meanings include "to suffer" or "to endure." It's in this sense that Christians refer to the Passion of Christ. Over time, it has come to have almost the opposite meaning. Passion now means a deep personal attraction to something—a strong affinity or enthusiasm that can lead to profound enjoyment and fulfillment. Passion is a form of love, which is why people who are in the Element will often say that they love what they do.

There are many sorts of love. There is love of family, romantic love, sexual love, love of friends, of places, of things and activities. In English, the word "love" is used to cover everything you're attracted to, from donuts to your fiancé. So what sort of love do you feel when you're in your Element?

Fortunately, some languages make finer distinctions that can help us here. In ancient Greek, for example, there are four words for love. *Agape* is a feeling of goodwill for humanity in general and for those we hold in high esteem. The closest word to this in English is "charity," in its original meaning of selfless love towards others. *Eros* is romantic love and sexual attraction for another person. *Storge* means the natural affection that parents have for their children and vice versa, and the love for others who are dear to us including the love between close friends. *Philia* is friendship and loyalty to others. It also means natural attraction to particular things or activities.

Philia is the origin of the English suffixes "-phil," "-phile" and "-philia," which indicate a special affinity for something, as in "bibliophile," a lover of books; "Francophile," a lover of all things French; or "chorophilia," a love of dancing. More improbably, there is also "dromophilia," a love of crossing streets; and "sesquipedalophilia," which, appropriately enough, is a love of long words.

It's difficult to separate completely the meanings of agape, eros, storge and philia. Since ancient times they've often been used in overlapping ways. Even so, philia is closest to what we usually have in mind when we talk about loving cooking, archaeology, athletics, entrepreneurship, teaching or whatever it is that fires our imaginations and stokes our energy. The key word here is *energy*. All life is energy: without energy there is no life. Passion is the power of positive spiritual energy.

Two Sorts of Energy

As you look for your Element it's useful to distinguish two sorts of energy, even though they're intimately related: physical energy and spiritual energy.

Your physical energy is related to the health of your body and how well you look after it. If you eat the wrong foods, drink too much alcohol, take certain sorts of drugs, have too little exercise or irregular sleep, eventually your body will let you know about it. If you have a physical disease, your energy will be impaired in some way. Levels of exertion affect it, too. If you run a marathon, it doesn't matter how fit you are, you'll have much less energy at the end of it than when you began. If you haven't, there's a large market for whatever you're taking.

But there are other factors that affect your physical energy whatever condition your body is in. They have to do with your motivation, with your moods and feelings, with your outlook on your life and with your sense of purpose. They have to do with your spirit. By "spirit," I mean your unique life force: the sense in which you might be in high spirits or low spirits.

During a typical day, your physical energy may rise and fall according to what you're doing and as your moods and feelings change. If you're doing something you love, by the end of the day you may be physically tired but spiritually energized. If you spend the day doing things you don't care for, you may be physically fine but feel spiritually low and find yourself reaching for a bottle of spirits. Passion is about what feeds your spiritual energy rather than consumes it.

My older brother Ian is a great musician. He's been playing drums in rock bands since he was fourteen and also plays keyboards and guitar at professional levels. Music is his main passion in life, but it's never been his main source of income. For that, he's depended on running his own businesses. Music has always run in parallel with his business life. Throughout his life, he's toured with bands and run his own, often playing gigs late into the evening and arriving home well after midnight after a long road trip knowing he had to get up early to get to the office for a full day's work. Even at the end of a long day, he'll be in his studio until the early hours, playing, listening and practicing. For Ian, life without music would be unimaginable. It's what feeds his spirit even when he's physically exhausted.

It's impossible to divide activities categorically into those that lift people's spirits and those that do not. For every activity you can think of, someone will love it and someone else will be allergic to it. I'm that way with shopping. I have friends (and family) who just love to shop. One of our friends loves it so much that she is considering taking on clients to help them buy clothes and furnishings. I couldn't imagine doing this. To start with, I'd be clueless and would lose any client after my first purchase. But I also get physically depressed in shops. The moment I cross the threshold of a clothes shop, I begin to lose the will to live. My shoulders fall, my eyes dull, and I have to sit down to support the heavy weight of my heart. While my soul is quietly gasping for air in most retail outlets, I see other people sucking in the same atmosphere with looks of exhilarated enchantment.

Name any activity and you'll find people who can't imagine doing anything else, and people who couldn't imagine anything worse. I asked this question on Twitter: "Who do you know that loves doing a job that you couldn't bear?" I was flooded with responses. The variety of answers illustrated the point perfectly. Several people immediately replied, "My proctologist!" It took some spiritual energy to move past the inevitable image that this response brought to mind. Proctologists are a vital part of the medical world. Colon cancer is the third most diagnosed cancer in both men and women, and early detection is hugely important. I don't want to think of a world without proctologists, and most proctologists will tell you that they love their job. That said, it's certainly not a profession that would suit everyone.

One woman said that she has a friend who absolutely loves his job of wading through sewers. Again, an essential part of modern society, admittedly not widely desired, and yet this person just loves it. Another woman wrote that the thought of mountaineering and trekking through jungles is her worst nightmare, and yet for someone else a life in the great outdoors would be a dream come true. She reminded me of the great British performer Marti Caine, who once told my wife, Thérèse, "If you can't do it in high heels, I'm not interested!"

Other jobs that many people couldn't imagine enjoying included accountants, lawyers, nurses and police officers. There were just as many people who said they love these roles. Interestingly, a common response was "teacher." Many said they love teaching; just as many said they wouldn't last a week in the job. Almost all the teachers who said how much they love their job said they have friends who can't imagine how they do it. One teacher put it this way:

"A question I'm often asked, mainly by the older students at school and several friends, is 'Why teaching? Why would you have that job?' I generally reply with another question: 'Why not? Why wouldn't I be teaching? Why wouldn't I be doing the thing that I actually love to do?' Rather like asking my father and grandfather, Why are they farming? They found a passion early on in life, something they are good at, and ran with it. Not to be rich, or wealthy, or considered highly by their peers, but simply because they love what they do. So much so they do not consider it even work: it's doing something that speaks directly to who they are. My granddad is now eighty-two and still goes out farming—at eighty-two! In wind, rain, snow and hail, with two titanium knees, two titanium hips and needing two titanium shoulders too! Is he mad? Has granddad lost his marbles? No. It's part of who he is, and to stop would be to lose something of himself."

The key point here is that finding your passion and being in your Element are about connecting to your own spiritual energies. Let's take one more example.

Guitar Hero, Artisan Division

Emily Cummins discovered her passions when she was very young. Randy Parsons took a little longer. When he was in high school, his friends were telling him that he was going to be a rock star. Growing up in the Seattle area, he was a very good guitarist who clearly stood out from his peers. By the time he graduated college, though, he was certain that he was never going to be playing to sold-out arenas, that he didn't have what it takes to become a breakout performer. He was passionate about music, but he saw no future in it. When he walked into the adult world, he walked away from his six-strings. Completely. He sold his guitars, joined the military, eventually took a job in law enforcement and didn't look back.

The only issue was that he didn't feel complete. "I was kind of happy," he told me, "but I think like most people, deep down inside something was missing. I just figured, 'This is life. I'll just keep my chin up and try to make the best of it.' I was somebody else now. It felt like when you know you're marrying the wrong person but you go through with it anyway. There was a voice of emptiness that I just shoved way back there. I tried to make the best of what I had, but there was that feeling that I wasn't a hundred percent. I spent five years with the city and there was always something calling me that I couldn't put my finger on, something telling me that this wasn't it."

Randy might have kept on this path for the rest of his life. He was good at what he did. His employers loved him. There were promotions in his future. He could have tried to convince himself that he was "somebody else" and that this person didn't need a passion to feel truly alive. Fortunately, it didn't play out that way.

One day, while he was taking a shower, "My entire future flashed in front of my eyes," he said. "It was such a gift because I got to see in a fraction of a second not only what I should be doing, but also how I should go about achieving it. I saw myself being a famous guitar maker and building guitars for my heroes. This vision was so powerful I was shaking. I had to dry off as fast as I could and drive down to the hardware store to buy some tools. I didn't even know what to buy. I had three hundred dollars on my debit card, and I bought a hundred-dollar little band saw, some glue, and a hammer. I ran home, went down to my basement, and turned it into a wood shop. I literally spent two years in that basement on my own, inventing how to make guitars."

Randy had no idea that he had the aptitude to be an internationally renowned luthier—he had never even done particularly well in shop class—but he had an unquenchable desire to make his vision in the shower come true. He spent all of his spare time over the next two years in his basement cutting wood. He'd get a potential guitar to a certain point, make a mistake, learn from the mistake, and start over on a new piece of wood. "My wife and my family were wondering why I kept not finishing them. I would say, 'I don't care about finishing these guitars. I take them as far as I can, and when I screw one up, I throw it away and continue.'"

At the end of the two years, he still hadn't finished a single guitar, but he felt that he'd learned enough to open a guitar repair shop within a local music store. He quit his job, cashed in his 401(k) and embarked on his new career. Meanwhile, he kept working at his craft, immersing himself in the guitar maker's life. Believing that flamenco guitars were the purest form of guitar making, he decided that he needed to eat a great deal of Mexican food and to learn to speak Spanish to put him in the right frame of mind. He hired a local college professor to tutor him in the language, and when the professor asked him why he wanted to learn Spanish, Randy told him. The professor stunned Randy when he said that he not only knew about the legendary luthier Boaz, whom Randy refers to as "a traveling gypsy rock star guitar maker," but also that Boaz had recently come to Tacoma to build a collection of special guitars that nearly no one knew how to make.

"The next day, I drove down to Tacoma and started working with him. Boaz took me from learning about wood to learning how to really do it. If I hadn't done the two years in my basement, I wouldn't have known what he was talking about. Because I went through that process, I got everything he said. He took me under his wing and taught me all of these lost art secrets, like how to put a piece of wood in your mouth and smell it to determine if it was ready enough for the guitar, if the sap inside had crystallized and was going to be good for tone."

Randy spent much of the next year learning from Boaz while building his repair business. He was as comfortable with the business side of his enterprise as he was with the craft. He liked creating a brand for himself, and he liked marketing his work. When the music store chain Guitar Center opened a location in Seattle, Randy saw the opportunity to dramatically grow his business.

"They had this empty warehouse next door. I told them I'd like to remodel a part of it since they weren't doing anything with it." The people at Guitar Center were resistant to the idea, but they agreed to let Randy look around. "I went in and took some pictures. By this point, I had designed my own business card; it was black with a red border stripe on the top. I took a picture of something I saw in the back corner of the warehouse. Someone had put up a big black tarp and on top of it was a red banner. It was my business card hanging in the warehouse! I decided that this was where my business was going to be." Within the month, Randy had set up his shop in the warehouse.

From there, Parsons Guitars built an international reputation. White Stripes guitarist Jack White was the first rock superstar to buy a guitar from Randy, and he even mentioned Randy by name in the Davis Guggenheim documentary *It Might Get Loud*. Since then, many others have called with commissions. "When I was a teenager, Jimmy Page was my god. Two years ago, I'm in L.A. in his hotel room giving him a guitar, and I'm currently building him another one." Meanwhile, Randy has a chain of five Parsons Guitars shops in the Seattle area.

Years ago, Randy Parsons had no idea that he had a passion for making guitars. Now, he is one of the world's great luthiers.

For him, the moral is inescapable. "You gotta find that thing that you love so much that you're gonna be the best at it. I didn't care if I was going to be poor or rich—I was gonna do this no matter. This was what was calling me. This was what made me happy. When I was cutting pieces of wood in the basement, I really felt that there was something grabbing my hand and showing me how to do it. There was no doubt in my mind that I was going where I was supposed to be going."

If you'd asked Randy Parsons when he was seventeen what he truly loved, he probably would have told you that he loved playing guitar. However, Randy had a deeper passion, one he hadn't fully explored when he was dreaming of being a rock star: he loved the physical artistry of the guitar itself. Once he uncovered this passion, he was able to create a lifestyle that allowed him to engage in this work every day. By being true to his passions, Randy Parsons was being true to himself, to his own spirit. So what is that exactly?

Being True to Your Spirit

We live in two worlds: the world of our own consciousness and the world of other people and events. In common sense, we accept that we each have our own essential "self." I know this to be true from my own experience of being alive. My own consciousness is often a constant flow of thoughts, feelings, sensations and moods. Like you, I'm capable of moving through many different levels of consciousness, voluntarily or involuntarily—from idling in front of a television, to focusing on a conversation that matters, to being lost in daydreams, to enjoying the closeness of my family, to trying to organize my ideas for this book.

Although they are all different, I don't doubt that there is a continuous "me," a "self," in here who is having these experiences and being conscious of them. I assume the same is true of you. What is this self? Are you conscious of it, or is your consciousness what it is? What is consciousness anyway?

In the most obvious sense, consciousness is what you lose when you fall asleep and what you get back when you wake up. In a deeper sense, your consciousness is essentially who you are; it is your spirit. There are three words that are often used in discussing aspects of the human spirit: "mind," "personality" and "consciousness." Defining them raises all kinds of complexities and they overlap in all sorts of ways, but let me say briefly what I mean by them here. By "mind," I mean the internal flow of thoughts, feelings and perceptions that you are aware of and aim to control in your waking hours. By "personality," I mean your general outlook and disposition to yourself and to the world around you. By "consciousness," I mean your fundamental awareness of your self as a living being.

Consciousness in this sense is a larger idea than either mind or personality. Both are part of your consciousness, but they are not the whole of it. In some ways, the continuous thoughts of your mind and the preoccupations of your personality can hinder your experience of deeper states of consciousness and obscure your true spirit.

I think of spiritual energy on three levels: the spirit *within* us, the spirit *between* us and the spirit *among* us. The first two don't require any metaphysical beliefs; the third one does.

The Spirit Within Us

It has been understood down the ages that each of us has a unique life force, an energy that animates our individual consciousness. There are many words in other languages for this spirit within us. In Hindu and yogic cultures, the Sanskrit word *prana* means vital life, the sustaining energy of all living beings. This is close to the traditional Chinese concept of *qi* or *chi*, which roughly translates as life force or energy flow. It also literally means "breath" or "air." In Japanese culture, the equivalent term is *ki*, in Polynesia, *mana*, and in Tibetan Buddhism *lung*, which also means "wind" or "breath." The Hebrew word *nephesh* is usually translated as "soul." Its literal meaning is "breath," too. The ancient Greek word *psyche*, as in psychology, is often used to refer to a person's mind and consciousness. The literal meaning of psyche is "life."

Exactly where your spirit comes from and how it relates to your body in general and to your brain in particular are perplexing questions that lie at the heart of science, philosophy and religion. The brain is infinitely complex. By one estimate, a cubic centimeter of the human brain—about the size of the tip of your little finger—contains more connections than there are stars in the Milky Way. As the neuroscientist David Eagleman put it, our attempts to understand our own brains are like a laptop computer turning its camera on its own circuits and trying to understand itself.

The fact that your consciousness does depend on the activity of your brain is fairly easy to demonstrate. In the English comedy series *Blackadder*, starring Rowan Atkinson, Blackadder is a scheming advisor in the sixteenth-century court of Queen Elizabeth I. In one episode, the Queen orders him to arrange the execution of one of her enemies. Blackadder later asks his dimwitted assistant Baldrick if the man is dead. Baldrick replies, "Well, we cut his head off. That normally does the trick . . ." So it does.

If even a small part of your brain is removed or damaged, it can permanently alter your mind, personality and consciousness. Drugs, alcohol and illness can all change the chemistry of the brain and how you think and feel. For some people, that's the whole point of taking them, of course.

Although your consciousness depends on your brain, it is not confined to it. Like the brain itself, consciousness is a function of your whole body. For example, we do not experience emotions as pangs and twitches inside our skulls, but as deep sensations in our limbs, gut and heart. You express your feelings and thoughts through physical gestures, facial expressions and tones of voice. Tension is often felt as physical symptoms: as butterflies in your stomach and pains in your neck. Some physical conditions are directly caused by mental states.

For some scientists and philosophers, the long processes of evolution and resulting complexity of our brains and bodies are enough to explain how consciousness came about. They see no need for any metaphysical explanations. Consciousness has simply evolved in human beings over millions of years, like opposing thumbs and binocular vision.

Even so, science is not yet close to agreeing on the nature of consciousness itself and what exactly makes you who you are. It doesn't account for the qualities of being human, for our delight in music, poetry and dance, for our passions for making beautiful objects and elaborate theories, or for the awkward euphoria of first love. Nor does it yet explain the many ways in which we engage with each other's spirits.

The Spirit Between Us

When you see someone that you like or love, you may feel your spirits lift. If you see someone you don't, your energy may drop.

Our everyday metaphors express this sense of connection with other people's spirits. We talk about being on the same "wavelength" with someone. Your energy may resonate so beautifully with them that you finish each other's sentences. Conversely, you may be so "out of tune" with someone that you misinterpret everything you say to each other. This feeling of connection or lack of connection with others is at the heart of being human and of being with and not just in the world around us.

Performers of all sorts talk about the peak moments when their energies align perfectly with those of audience. The guitarist Eric Clapton says that it's essential that artists and audience "surrender" during a performance. "I can't really explain what it's like except in a physical sense," he's said. "It's a massive rush of adrenaline, which comes at a certain point. Usually it's a sharing experience; it's not something I could experience on my own. . . . It's not even just the musicians: it's everyone that's involved in the whole experience. Everyone in that place seems to unify at one point. It's when you get that completely harmonic experience, where everyone is hearing exactly the same thing without any interpretation whatsoever or any kind of angle. They're all transported toward the same place. . . . You could call it unity, which is a very spiritual word for me. Everyone is one at that point, at that specific point in time, not for very long. Of course, the minute you become aware of that, it's gone."

Our connections with other people's energies don't require us to be in the same physical space. A mother may know her child's distress without being in the same room. At a more general level, we're all affected by shifts in fashion, in cultural values and habits, and in ways of thinking across whole populations. The psychologist Carl Jung had these sorts of dynamics in mind when he coined the term "collective unconscious." The Germans call this Zeitgeist: the spirit of the times.

The Spirit Among Us

For some secular thinkers, and all religious ones, your spirit is much more than the chemical simmering of your brain and nervous systems. For all faith traditions, your spirit is not a by-product of biology but part of larger energy beyond our everyday understanding. In the Judeo-Christian tradition, your "soul" is an enduring essence that continues after the death of your body. In Buddhism, the term that's closest to soul is *anatta*, which translates as "no soul" or "no self." This isn't quite the opposite that it seems. Buddhism accepts a transcendent element to your being that continues after death but believes that it is continuously evolving into new forms. Hindus use the Sanskrit word *aatma*, which broadly means the individual self that is related to and part of Brahman, the Supreme Self of the Universe. Jainism talks of *jiva*, which equates to the individual living being compared with Shiva or Vishnu, the Supreme Being. Islam uses the term *ruhi*.

Eckhart Tolle draws from many spiritual traditions to argue that the conscious mind, or ego, as he calls it, is a very small part of who we really are. And our own spirits in turn are only part of a greater divine energy. To connect with your true self and with the divine, you have to calm the demands of your mind and ego. "Once there is a certain degree of Presence, of still and alert attention in human beings' perceptions," Tolle writes, "they can sense the divine life essence, the one indwelling consciousness or spirit in every creature, every life form, recognize it as one with their own essence and so love it as themselves. Until this happens however most humans see only the outer forms, unaware of the inner essence, just as they are unaware of their own essence and identify only with their own physical and psychological form."

This experience of transcendence is at the heart of many systems of belief. Whether you believe in a metaphysical dimension to your spirit is a personal matter for you. However you conceive of it, being true to your spirit in the here and now is in part what finding your Element is all about. Why does this matter?

Feeling Positive

For the past three hundred years, the dominant view in Western culture has been that intelligence has to do with certain sorts of logic and reason. Feelings were thought to be disruptive and distracting. Partly because of this, the history of psychology and psychiatry in the last hundred years has been mainly about emotional disorders and mental illness. Science is now discovering two things that artists and spiritual leaders have always understood: that our feelings and emotions are vital to the quality of our lives and that there are intimate relationships between how we think and feel.

There is a difference between negative feelings and positive feelings. Negative feelings include hate, anger, fear and contempt. Positive feelings include joy, love, compassion, happiness and delight. George E. Vaillant is a psychoanalyst and research psychiatrist at Harvard University. In *Spiritual Evolution* he sets out a sustained defense of positive emotions and their role in human well-being. He notes that modern science has come to accept the importance of emotions but, even so, the emphasis remains on the negative rather than positive emotions. In 2004, "the leading American text, *The Comprehensive Textbook of Psychiatry*, half a million lines in length, devotes 100 to 600 lines each to shame, guilt, terrorism, anger, hate and sin; thousands of lines to depression and anxiety; but only five lines to hope, one line to joy and not a single line to faith, compassion and forgiveness."

From an evolutionary perspective, the negative emotions orig-inate in the oldest parts of the human brain and are dedicated to individual survival. The positive emotions evolved later and are what bind us to each other as human beings. "The positive emo-tions are more expansive and help us to broaden and build," Vail-lant says. "They widen our tolerance, expand our moral compass and enhance our creativity. . . . Experiments document that while negative emotions narrow attention . . . positive emotions, espe-cially joy, make thought patterns far more flexible, creative, inte-grative and efficient."

Dwelling in negative feelings can damage your physical and spiritual well-being. They can cause stress in your body and dis-tress in your spirit. Connecting with positive emotions has the opposite effect of improving your physical health and spiritual well-being. Vaillant attributes our human sense of spirituality in part to the unique nature of the human brain and to our inborn capacities for positive emotions. For thirty-five years, Vaillant di-rected the Harvard Study of Adult Development. "In the first thirty years leading the study," he says, "I learned that positive emotions were intimately connected to mental health. In the last ten years, I have come to appreciate that positive emotions cannot be distinguished from what people understand as spirituality."

Being in your Element is about connecting with and dwelling in the positive feelings that express and fulfill your own spiritual energies. One way of discovering the roots of these feelings, and of finding your Element, is through the practices of mindfulness. These practices draw on the principles and techniques of medita-tion that I suggested in chapter one.

Positive Psychology is a movement to promote the importance of connecting with our positive feelings. One of the aims is to pro-mote a greater sense of mindfulness. The aim is to go beyond the daily chatter of your mind, and the endless agenda of tasks and anxieties that often drive it, to a deeper sense of your own being and purpose. In *Fully Present: The Science, Art, and Practice of Mindfulness*, Susan Smalley and Diana Winston argue that, "Learning to live mindfully does not mean living in a perfect world, but rather living a full and contented life in a world in which both joys and challenges are givens. Although mindfulness does not remove the ups and downs of life, it changes how experiences like losing a job, getting a divorce, struggling at home or at school, births, marriages, illnesses, death and dying influence you and how you influence the experience. . . . In other words, mindfulness changes your relationship to life."

The practice of mindfulness has been shown to promote many positive benefits that include:

- reducing stress
- reducing chronic physical pain
- boosting the body's immune system to fight disease
- coping with painful life events such as the death of a loved one or a major illness
- dealing with negative emotions
- increasing self-awareness to detect harmful patterns of thought
- improving attention and concentration
- enhancing positive emotions including happiness and compassion
- increasing interpersonal skills and relationships
- reducing addictive behaviors
- enhancing performance in work, sports or academics
- stimulating and releasing creativity
- changing the actual structure of our brains.

The practice of mindfulness draws on many ancient principles of meditation. It can have many benefits in itself. It can also be among the ways in which you can connect with your true spirit and your positive emotions. In these ways, it can also help you to find your Element.

Frequently Asked Questions

Against this background, let me come back to the questions I'm frequently asked about passion that I listed at the beginning of this chapter.

WHAT IF I HAVE NO PASSIONS?

There are plenty of people who don't know what their passions are, but it's a rare person who has none. There are people who have an unusually limited range of feelings. There are sociopaths and psychopaths who lack some of the usual human emotions, especially empathy for the feelings of others. There is a much larger group of people who, through trauma or depression, have lost touch with their positive feelings. But being cut off from your passions or not knowing what they may be is different from not having any to start with.

The conductor of the Boston Philharmonic, Benjamin Zander, makes a similar point about people who say they are tone deaf: "An amazing number of people think they're tone deaf. Or, as I hear a lot of, 'My husband is tone deaf!' Actually, you cannot be tone deaf. Nobody is tone deaf. If you were tone deaf . . . you couldn't tell the difference between somebody from Texas and somebody from Rome. If your mother calls you on the telephone and says 'hello,' you not only know who it is, you know what mood she's in. Everyone has a fantastic ear."

Interestingly, Zander also says: "Everybody loves classical music, it's just that many people haven't found out about it yet." I believe this is true of many of your potential passions. The point is to keep looking.

WHAT IF I LOVE SOMETHING I'M NOT GOOD AT?

Whatever your aptitudes, the greatest source of achievement is passion. Aptitude matters, but passion often matters more. The reason I didn't make progress on the piano or guitar was that I didn't have a passion for them. If you love doing something, you'll be constantly drawn to get better at it.

Just as you live in two worlds, there are broadly two types of motivation: external and internal. You may do something because of external demands in the world around you—because it pays the bills, solves a practical problem, or is required by your job or education. Or you may do something because you have a strong internal motivation—because of the inherent pleasure, enjoyment or fulfillment it gives you. We achieve our best when we have strong internal motivations.

Teresa Amabile is one of the world's leading researchers in creativity. She confirms the powerful relationship between achievement and passion. "People are more creative when they're passionate about what they're doing," says Amabile, "when they feel personally involved in it, excited about it, and when they have a deeper level of enjoyment. Even though at any one moment they may not feel like they're having fun because it's really hard work, they still have a deep level of attachment to that work." If you want to do your most creative work, she says, "You shouldn't focus solely on what your talents are and decide that you can't do creative work in a particular area because you see other people who are more talented than you."

You do need some aptitude for what you want to do, but passion is what makes the real difference. After all, as Amabile says, "There are plenty of extremely talented people who never do anything, really."

By the way, you may be better than you think at what you love. You may underestimate your talent because you set unreasonably high standards for yourself. Having high standards is good, provided you're not immobilized by self-criticism. If you've just taken up painting, there's no point comparing your first efforts with the mature work of the masters of the Renaissance. Mastering any discipline takes time and effort. If you're on the right path, much of the pleasure is in the process. You should be inspired by those who are further down the road than you are, not discouraged by how far you have to go. If you love what you do, you should enjoy the journey of improvement and not be frustrated by having to make it.

WHAT IF WHAT I LOVE IS MORALLY DUBIOUS?

I am sometimes asked if it's all right to follow your passion if it's for something unsavory or harmful, like arson or cruelty. I'm sure you can think of your own examples. No, it's not. Let me qualify that answer. All my arguments for the Element have to be framed within an acceptable moral code. Moral standards can vary enormously between cultures and over time. These are matters we all need to think through for ourselves and decide on what's acceptable and what is not. In my moral universe, one of the purposes of having moral values is for us to avoid harm to other people and to create conditions where communities can live together freely and harmoniously. Passion, that is, has to be related to compassion. If your Element involves undermining the happiness of other people or doing them actual damage, I don't approve of it and you shouldn't expect many other people to, either. Real happiness, as I will argue later on, is an internal state that is often enhanced by looking beyond ourselves to the well-being of others.

WHO'S GOING TO CLEAN THE TOILETS?

I often hear people say something like, "Finding your Element is fine, but who's going to collect the trash, work on assembly lines and clean the toilets?" I have two responses. The first is that the vast differences in personal passions mean that you should hesitate before judging what other people love to do. At a book signing in Minneapolis, a man in his forties told me that his mother had been an office cleaner for more than twenty years and she absolutely loved it. She worked evenings and looked forward to it all day. She loved the process of cleaning in itself and the feeling of satisfaction at the end of her shift when everything was neat, organized and in good order. On top of that, this was the one time in the day that she had completely to herself away from the demands of home; a time when she could think for herself and be herself.

Of course, there are people doing work they don't like. Remember what Dr. Schwartz said about the job dissatisfaction percentage. And it may not be possible for everyone to make a living from what they love to do. If you are in a job that you dislike, it's even more important to spend some part of your day doing something that fulfills you and connects to your true passions. While not everyone can become financially rich through their Element, everyone is entitled to be enriched by it.

HOW WILL I KNOW WHEN I'VE FOUND MY ELEMENT?

Finding your Element can be a little like falling in love. The original title I had in mind for *The Element* was *Epiphany*. An epiphany is a sudden realization—a moment of unexpected revelation. I liked that title because the book is about discovering your true spirit and the difference that makes in your life. "Epiphany" seemed to capture that sense of transformation. We changed the title for two reasons. The first is that "epiphany" has religious overtones. Although there is a spiritual dimension to my argument, it's not a religious one. The second reason is more important.

For some people, finding their Element is like love at first sight. I spoke a couple of years ago at a large educational conference in the American Midwest that was held in the banqueting hall of a casino. (I don't know, either.) I talked about how some people fall instantly in love with something. A man in his mid-sixties put his hand up and said that was exactly what had happened to him. When he was in his early twenties, he was on his way to becoming an engineer. He had a friend whose father ran a restaurant and he'd arranged to meet him there before going out for the evening. His friend told him to come in through the kitchen at the back of the building. He'd never been in a restaurant kitchen before. The moment he crossed the threshold, he was overwhelmed. He was captivated by the energy—the clatter, the flaming stoves, the smells, the constant cursing and above all the intense focus on the food. He decided there and then that this was the life he wanted. He went on to train as a chef and to open a series of restaurants of his own. When I met him, he'd been happily immersed in the restaurant business for more than forty years. Someone else might have dodged through the kitchen as fast as possible to escape the mayhem. As they say, if you can't stand the heat stay out of the kitchen.

I once asked a radio interviewer how he started in broadcasting. He'd had a similar experience to the chef's. In the ninth grade, he and his class were taken on a school visit to a local radio station. While the rest of his class merely enjoyed the visit, he thought it was magical. As soon as he walked into the studio, he was enchanted by it and knew then what he wanted to do with his life.

For some people like these, finding their Element is an epiphany. But not everyone has this "road to Damascus" experience. For others it's like falling in love over time.

I met Marsha at an event in Chicago. She was in her early forties and thanked me for *The Element*, which she said she had read and reread. When she was at school she'd had trouble reading. Then one of her teachers took an interest in her and recommended books that she thought she'd like. Gradually, she became hooked on reading and spent more and more time in the library. Over time she began to dream of becoming a school librarian. Now she is, and she loves every day of her work. Her real job she says is not organizing the books but connecting children to the books she thinks they'll love. She can't believe how lucky she is to be doing what she calls the best job in the world. Every day she gets to be among books and to inspire children to read and love them, too. She's delighted with herself and her life.

As you look for your Element, you may encounter something you've never done before and have an epiphany. Equally, you may discover that you've already been doing what you love for a long time without realizing it, like falling in love with an old friend. Of course, discovering that you love something that you've been taking for granted is an epiphany all of its own.

My wife, Thérèse, had that experience. She has recently published her first novel, *India's Summer*. She'd been writing for most of her life, but never focused on it as her principal passion or work. It was something she did alongside everything else she had to do. Those of us who are close to her always saw her talent, probably more clearly than she did. Eventually, she did begin to immerse herself in writing and fell in love with it. Here's how she puts it:

"I am at a new and very exciting point in my life. For the first time I have something tangible to show for my work. I've written a novel and that's now been published. Never before have I had so much positive affirmation, so many congratulations, so much delight in what I have achieved, and yet this feels like the easiest thing I have ever done.

"Bring on the standing ovation for the years spent teaching, raising my family, running a business, creating a home, caring for my parents, and supporting my husband's work. A round of applause, thank you, for the days spent cleaning and cooking, driving back and forth to school playgrounds, and dealing with all of the crises that happen along the way. Let's hear it for the thirty-five-year marriage and the friendships that have survived the years. Yes I am appreciated and loved, and yes I know I have done my best and had a productive and exciting life. I am rewarded on a daily basis by all of that love. Even so, I get a tremor of excitement at the thought of holding a completed project in my hands.

"Writing a novel has been one of the most satisfying, rewarding, pleasurable things I have ever done. It took me into a world of my own creation, where I was totally in control. When one of my characters went on an adventure, I went along for the ride, curious to see where that would take me. I discovered my only limitations were self-imposed. I wrote for the guilt-free pleasure of being locked in a world of my own imagination, without thought for whether it would make money, get published, or flop. I wrote whenever I could and probably at one of the busiest and most stressful times of my life. I wrote instead of shopping or reading or doing any of the many other things that usually give me space and time for myself.

"The more I turned up, the more easily the words flowed. I could hear my 'voice' getting stronger. There came a point where I wanted someone to share what I'd written and as a result I became more confident with my writing and more confident in myself, thrilled to learn that my friends had escaped into this fantasy I had created.

"I had no idea when I started out where this would lead. I still don't. What I do know is that once I committed fully to writing *India's Summer*, the project took on a life of its own. I used to think that what I needed more than anything else was time. What I have learned is that time expands to fill the space available.

"Now I'm working on the sequel. Something tells me I am not yet done with my protagonist."

Sometimes finding your Element is a sudden inspiration and sometimes it comes over you gradually. The result is the same. Your life is transformed by a different sense of engagement, satisfaction, and purpose.

By the way, changing the title of the book from *Epiphany* to *The Element* was not a good idea in every way. I spoke at the TED conference in 2006 and mentioned then that I was working on a book called *Epiphany*. That talk went on to be seen by millions of people around the world. Its popularity has done wonders for the sales of books called *Epiphany* that I've had absolutely nothing to do with. There's a moral in there somewhere.

Choosing Your Path

In some almost tangible way, finding and exploring your passion puts you on a different path—a path that, while hardly free of difficulty or hardship, seems easier to take. Joseph Campbell coined the phrase "follow your bliss" because the Sanskrit word *ananda* captured for him the essence of leaping toward transcendence. In his famous interviews with Bill Moyers that led to the book and PBS series *The Power of Myth,* Campbell elaborated on this phrase. He said that if you follow your bliss, "You put yourself on a kind of track that has been there all the while, waiting for you, and the life that you ought to be living is the one you are living. When you can see that, you begin to meet people who are in your field of bliss, and they open doors to you. I say, follow your bliss and don't be afraid, and doors will open where you didn't know they were going to be."

I've seen this happen many times: when you pursue what truly inspires you, opportunities open up that you might never have imagined. You gravitate toward people who share your passion, your combined efforts create a higher state of energy and proximity to these people increases the chance of your taking the pursuit to a new level—the opening of doors of which Campbell speaks. Campbell likens this to being helped by "invisible hands." It's impossible to avoid the spiritual connotation there, and depending on your inclination you might interpret that in any number of ways. What seems clear, regardless of how you look at it, is that following your bliss, or exploring your passions—Paulo Coelho calls it the personal legend—makes the world more alive for you and makes you more alive within it.

Ultimately, the two most important questions to ask yourself in the search for your passion are: what do you love, and what do you love about it? With that in mind, let's return to the exercise that you started at the beginning of the chapter.

Exercise Eight: What Draws You In?

- Look at the three groups of activities that you created in Exercise Seven.
- Is it possible for you to put the things you love in any order of priority—say a top five or ten?
- Take each of these groups and ask yourself what you do or don't love about them. How have you experienced them and in what context?
- Look particularly at the things that you love to do. What is it you love about them? Can you imagine applying them in other ways or another context you haven't tried yet?
- Can you imagine ways in which the things you don't enjoy could be applied in ways that you might?

These questions are simple, though coming to the answers might not be. Still, if you can truly identify what gives you consistent joy, you'll have a very good sense of what your passion might be. And if you can truly identify what specifically you love about this thing, you'll be that much further along. Here are some other questions for you to reflect on as we continue:

- What sorts of activities lift your spirits and feed your energy?
- What activities make time disappear for you?
- Have you ever had an epiphany?
- What was it and what have you done about it?

- Are there things that you've always loved to do but not focused on fully?
- What are the reasons for that?
- When do you feel that you are being most true to your own spirit?

CHAPTER FIVE

What Makes You Happy?

How happy are you? Will finding your Element make you happier? This chapter looks at what happiness really is, at what it takes to achieve it, and how finding your Element is fundamental to it.

Ask people what they want in their lives and most will say they want to be happy. This is true in all parts of the world and in every sort of culture. People may say that they want other things, like successful careers, good health, being in love, having more money or a family. The assumption is that having these will make them happier. Of course, some people are naturally miserable and say they're not interested in being happy at all. I don't believe them any more than I believe those who say they have no passions or that they're tone deaf. Other people may feel very distant from happiness for a time. They may be depressed, bereaved or suffering. But for most people, much of the time, being happy is a sustaining purpose and aspiration. So how does being in your Element make you happy and what can you do to make it happen?

Exercise Nine: How Happy Are You?

Before we look further at the nature of happiness, pause for a while and think about how you define happiness for yourself and about how happy you are now. Do this by making a mind map of happiness:

- Write the word "Happiness" in the center of a large sheet of paper and draw a circle around it.
- Think about all the things that you associate with happiness and write them down.
- Using different colors, draw lines away from the circle for each of these things, and write a headline word along each line. If you associate happiness with having a lot of money, you might have a line with the word "wealth" and so on.
- Draw branching lines from each of the main lines to show what else you associate with each of these main ideas. If you associate relationships with happiness, you might have branching lines for "good friends," "having a family" and so on.
- When you've filled it in as much as you can, look at the whole map and ask yourself how you're doing now in relation to each of these areas. You can use words like "very well," "average," "not so good" or come up with your own scale of evaluation. You could use a color code instead of words, if you prefer.
- Finally, ask yourself how your current ratings compare with five, ten and twenty years ago—according to how old you are, of course.

- Are you happier in some areas of your life than others? Are you more or less happy now than at other times in your life? In making these assessments, what do you think happiness really is? What do you think it takes to increase it?

The Unhappy Truth

Although most people say that they want to be happy, there is mounting evidence that the majority of people are not. One of the paradoxes of our times is that on the whole, people seem less happy than twenty or thirty years ago in spite of rising levels of affluence over the same period.

In 2003, Dan Baker published *What Happy People Know*. Based on long experience of working with adults from all sorts of backgrounds, he discusses what does and does not make people happy. True happiness, he says, is relatively rare. "More people think that happiness is common among others. In reality, happiness . . . in modern America is even scarcer now than in earlier less affluent times. In terms of happiness, America is going downhill even as our affluence has blossomed . . . The more we've attained, the emptier we've become."

There are several ways of assessing levels of unhappiness. They include levels of disengagement from work or education, levels of depression, use of drugs and alcohol and, most bleakly, of suicide. At one end of the spectrum there are the huge numbers of people who are chronically disengaged at work or in school because they find it all pointless and unfulfilling. At the other are the jaw-dropping numbers who are critically addicted to alcohol, tobacco or other drugs as a way of stimulating or suppressing their feelings.

According to one study, almost half of the adults in the United

States have little enthusiasm for life and are not actively or pro-
ductively engaged in the world. There are equally disturbing figures for other countries and regions of the world, from Europe to
Asia. The personal, social and economic costs of these levels of
disengagement are extremely high. Sonja Lyubomirsky is a respected psychologist and author. She argues that these high levels
of disengagement help to explain "why the desire to be happier is
felt not just by the clinically depressed but by a wide range of
us . . . from those who are not as happy as we'd like to be, who
sense we're not quite thriving, to those who may be doing quite
well yet want more—more joy, more meaning in life, more stimulating relationships and jobs."

Depression is becoming an increasingly serious problem. In
the United Kingdom, for example, prescriptions for antidepres-
sant drugs have risen by more than forty percent in the past four
years. This is not a uniquely British problem. On the contrary,
the World Health Organization predicts that by 2020 depression
will be the second leading cause of death in the world, affecting
thirty percent of all adults. Many experts believe that depression
has become an epidemic. By some estimates, "clinical depression
is ten times more likely to torment us than it did a century ago."

Of those suffering from depression, an alarming number
commit suicide. Numbers of suicides have increased in the last
thirty years, and especially among young people between fifteen
and twenty-five. Perhaps as many as twenty times more people
attempt suicide than actually succeed.

There are as many reasons for depression and disengagement as
there are individuals who feel them. But there are some general
trends and causes, too. They include the high expectations of material goods and standards of living that are incessantly promoted

through the media. The financial insecurities unleashed by the 2008 recession have also shaken the confidence of people around the world. And then there are the profound changes in family and community life and the growing emphasis on individual achievement. These can all add to a sense of personal insecurity and risk. Ironically, the so-called social media may also be adding their own pressures. Although they have far more connections than ever online, many young people feel they have fewer real friends they can turn to for actual company and comfort when they need it.

On top of all of this, one of the most fundamental reasons why so many people feel unhappy is that happiness itself is so widely misunderstood.

Looking in the Wrong Place?

There are many misconceptions of happiness. They show up in the many "if only" statements people make about being happy. "I'd be happy, if only I won the lottery; had a big house; were married; were divorced; had children; didn't have children; had a better body; had better body parts; a different face; a different job." I don't mean to say that none of these things would make you happy. I could make my own list and would be delighted if some of them came true. But often our images of what will make us happy are illusions, not visions.

Many people think that having more money will make them happy. When I started my postgraduate studies in London in 1972, I was living on a stipend of three thousand pounds a year. (In 2013, it would be the equivalent of possibly twenty thousand U.S. dollars.) This was a fortune compared to what I'd been living on as an undergraduate. Inevitably, it wasn't enough, and I wound up bouncing a check. I had a wonderful bank manager, Mr. Parminter. But for him, you might never have heard from me again. My next job paid half again as much, forty-eight hundred pounds. I went to see Mr. Parminter to tell him our troubles were over. He said he doubted this and quoted an old adage in banking that spending rises with income. He was perfectly right, of course. The ideal amount of money that most people want is more than they have now. Like the end of the rainbow, the optimum income seems to be just ahead of where we actually are.

Money matters, of course. If you have too little money to meet the basic needs of life, you have a problem that can make you miserable. But the opposite proposition—that having a lot of money will make you happy—is not reliably true. The United States is by far the richest country in the world. It's also one of the least happy ones. Between 1973 and 2002, gross domestic product (GDP) in the United Kingdom grew by eighty percent. Over the same period, life satisfaction flatlined.

Many of the things we assume will make us happy forever only make us happy for a while. In *Stumbling on Happiness,* psychologist Dan Gilbert says that, "We think that money will bring lots of happiness for a long time and actually it brings a little happiness for a short time." Dan Baker agrees: "The myth that money brings you happiness is one of the happiness traps," he says. In a study of 792 well-off adults, "more than half reported that wealth didn't bring them more happiness and half of those with assets greater than $10 million said that money brought more problems than it solved."

For many people, a life of leisure and pleasure seems the ideal road to perpetual happiness. There are good reasons to doubt it. For people who have been active and energetic, retirement can be a time of boredom and frustration. For those with the means to support it, a life of constant "leisure" usually brings its own sense of ennui.

There's a big difference between temporary pleasures and being fundamentally happy. All kinds of experiences can make you feel good for a time: your favorite food, chocolate, partying, a great book, music that you love, watching your favorite baseball team win a game or having an intimate evening with your lover. You can make your own list. But when the hormones subside and the morning breaks, you may still feel as unfulfilled deep down as you did before the party started. You may be happy for a time, but sustained happiness depends on having a deeper sense of fulfillment. So what is it, and where and how does being in your Element contribute to your long-term happiness?

Having a Purpose

Yasmin Helal is a professional basketball player in Cairo, and quite an accomplished one. She played with the Egyptian national team for nearly a decade. She's also had a career as a biomedical engineer, and again she was rather skilled at that. Yasmin is good at a number of things that she also enjoys. She didn't discover the thing that truly makes her happy, though, until she was driving in her car, coming home from a festival, and some beggars came up to her.

"I did very well with my studies and I was doing very well at work," she told me. "Everything was so cool. Then I was stopped by three street kids who were asking me for money. Luckily I found some in my car that I was planning to donate to something else, and I gave that money to them. They asked for more, and I said I didn't have more but to come back the next day and I would have more then. I had some feelings of guilt because I live in the same city as those people and yet I had no idea what their needs were and that a little money could change their lives. At the same time, I felt gratitude because I felt I was so lucky to have a good education, have a house, have parents, and stuff like that."

She'd been living among those far less fortunate for most of her life, but the sweep of her other pursuits kept her from noticing what their experiences were like. As it happens, she'd recently been reading John Wood's book, *Leaving Microsoft to Change the World*, about how the tech millionaire quit to create a foundation that has built schools and libraries for the impoverished. When she returned to bring the kids more money, probably astonishing them in the process, she made good on her promise and came away with a true inspiration.

"I decided to start an initiative to sponsor the financing of underprivileged kids to go to school. For the next four months, I went to poor places nearby trying to understand the needs of these people. I went to public schools to learn how much money was needed. Eventually, I came up with this initiative. After, I learned there was a new problem because kids were going to school at ages eight and nine without knowing how to read and write. The schools needed to pay extra money to the teachers to teach these kids after school. At the time, I was supported by three amazing individuals. We started our own foundation that would make my initiative bigger and make it sustainable. We found we could support other initiatives with the same mindset. We designed a parallel track next to the schooling. We developed a character-building program. We developed creative arts. We started exposing the kids outside of their area, to know their country to get to be proud of it and proud of our ancestors.

"I had to make sure that the money was going to the right

place. I wouldn't give the money to the people, but instead I would pay the fees to the schools, buy the uniforms, and whatever, and deliver them back to the people."

Yasmin found that there were few people in her circle who understood why this had become so important to her. "Most people felt that there were so many kids who needed help that I'd never be able to make any progress. People didn't know why I was doing this. They felt that if I wanted to contribute, I could volunteer for an NGO or make a donation. The only support I got was in the form of money. No one was ready to help me do it."

All of her assistance came from outside of this group, but that didn't prevent her from moving forward with the mission that gave her a greater sense of enjoyment than any she'd experienced before.

"As soon as I started this project, I found new purpose. I decided to quit my engineering job. It was amazing. I did this three months after I started the project. The company I was working for asked me to stay on for a month. I kept going there physically, but my mind and heart were elsewhere. I decided at that point that I would never again do something unless it contributed to people's development."

With the help of three other social entrepreneurs, Yasmin's mission has evolved into the NGO The Taleeda Foundation, whose first initiative is Educate-Me, which is "aimed at enabling underprivileged children to pursue their dreams through education, value setting, and character building." It's hard work and it's an uphill battle, especially in a country going through the changes Egypt is going through. Yasmin perseveres and thrives, though. Because it makes her happy.

Yasmin's story points to an important principle. The power of being in your Element is enhanced when it nurtures within you a greater sense of purpose. Having a purpose in life is the wellspring of sustained happiness.

What Is Happiness?

Happiness is not a material state: it is a spiritual one. It is an internal state of well-being. Sonja Lyubomirsky puts it this way: "Happiness is the experience of joy, contentment and well-being combined with a sense that life is good and worthwhile." True happiness is very different from the ephemeral feelings that come from sudden good fortune. According to Dr. Andrew Weil, "Happiness that comes from winning a bet or from another stroke of good luck is temporary and does not change the set point of our emotional variability," he notes. "Besides, as we all discover, fortune is fickle. If we hitch our moods to it, we are signing up for lows as powerful as any highs." Weil argues that emotional well-being is just as important as physical well-being and that we need to create the conditions that allow us to be happy through circumstances within our control. "Happiness arises spontaneously from sources within us," he says. "Seeking it outside ourselves is counterproductive."

When Weil talks about stretches of true happiness in his own life, he talks about having "a deep knowing that I was all right, on the right track, doing what I had been put here for. . . . I had much to be happy about in the usual sense, much good fortune, but the deeper feeling came from knowing that I was the person I was supposed to be, uniquely equipped to navigate the world and meet any challenges I might confront." In other words, he felt true happiness when he was in his Element.

Being happy is about engaging your positive emotions. Doing this benefits your whole being: physical and spiritual. Dan Baker puts it this way: "In the ultimate analysis human beings have only two primal feelings: fear and love. Fear compels us to survive and love enables us to thrive . . . Positive feelings increase dopamine and have beneficial effects on the body, especially on our cardiovascular systems. Stress and anxiety have the opposite effect."

One of the most important things you can do as you try to find your Element is to pay careful attention to your emotional states. Is there something you do that consistently elevates your spirits? When do you experience stretches of real joy? Remember that one of the primary ways that Brian Schwartz helps his clients sort through their interests is by identifying how good they feel when embarking on them. It is critical to identify this as you try to figure out what you're meant to do.

The Meaning of Happiness

There is a myth that being happy means being constantly cheerful. Martin Seligman is known as the Father of Positive Psychology. In 2003, he published *Authentic Happiness*, which sets out the case for a life of sustained happiness and the principles and practices for achieving it. He identifies three different elements of happiness: positive emotions, engagement and meaning. Positive emotions are what we feel. Engagement is about flow: "being one with the music, time stopping, and the loss of self-consciousness during an absorbing activity." The third element of happiness is meaning. "The pursuit of engagement and the pursuit of pleasure are often solitary, solipsistic endeavors. Human beings . . . want meaning and purpose in life." Typically that means "serving something that you believe is bigger than the self." Feeling you're doing something meaningful doesn't guarantee happiness, but it tends to be difficult to find happiness unless you feel that what you're doing is significant in some way.

Perhaps no one ever captured the value of finding meaning in your life more effectively than Viktor Frankl. An acclaimed psychotherapist in the thirties and forties, the Austrian Frankl was imprisoned in concentration camps for more than two and a half years. During this time, Frankl endured degradations and hardships—his mother, father and wife died in camps—that would have crushed nearly anyone's soul. He saw hundreds of his fellow prisoners, so many of whom were going through the same things as he, die in spirit before the Nazis murdered them. Frankl somehow managed to survive, largely because he never succumbed to complete despair.

In his landmark book, *Man's Search for Meaning*, Frankl described the horrors he endured in the camp. But he also described how he emerged from the experience with a heightened respect for humanity and of the power of hope and ideas to combat the worst hardships and inspire the greatest achievements. In writing the book, he says, "I had wanted simply to convey to the reader by way of concrete example that life holds a potential meaning under any conditions, even the most miserable ones . . . And I thought that if the point were demonstrated in a situation as extreme as that in a concentration camp, my book might gain a hearing. I therefore felt responsible for writing down what I had gone through, for I thought it might be helpful to people who are prone to despair."

When Frankl was finally liberated from the camps, he

founded the branch of psychotherapy known as logotherapy. The core doctrine is that finding meaning is a driving force in every life. "We can discover this meaning in life in three different ways," Frankl wrote: "(1) by creating a work or doing a deed; (2) by experiencing something or encountering someone; and (3) by the attitude we take toward unavoidable suffering." Logotherapy has been used to treat patients dealing with depression, anxiety and even terminal illness.

Whatever your circumstances may be, in many ways finding your Element is, above anything else, about finding meaning and purpose in your life. If you feel that a pursuit has meaning, you are likely to engage in it at an entirely different level. How much easier is it to do something, and how much more lightly does the time pass, if you feel that doing it has true meaning? If you feel that what you're doing matters to yourself or to the people around you, you're much more likely to enjoy doing it.

Yasmin Helal enjoyed playing basketball and her work at biomedical engineering. Either of these things could have been her Element, but it turned out that it was something else entirely. From the moment she decided to start Educate-Me, she could barely think of doing anything else. For the first time in her adult life, she believed that what she was doing was genuinely meaningful. She was convinced that she was meant to help people less fortunate, and her work with Educate-Me finally gave her that outlet.

Happiness and Well-Being

It's possible of course to be happy in one part of your life and not in others. For this reason, it's important to think of happiness within the broader context of your life as a whole.

In 2011 Martin Seligman published *Flourish*, the much-anticipated sequel to his book *Authentic Happiness*. In *Flourish* he says that there are serious limitations to his earlier arguments. Focusing only on happiness is too narrow, he says: happiness should be seen as part of a larger concept of well-being. Well-being has five measurable elements. To the three elements of happiness—positive emotions, engagement and meaning—he adds relationships and achievement. It is well-being, not happiness, says Seligman, that is the proper topic of positive psychology.

Scientists with the Gallup Organization have been exploring the demands of a life well lived since the mid-twentieth century. More recently, in partnership with leading economists, psychologists and other scientists, they began to explore the common elements of well-being that transcend cultures in more than one hundred and fifty countries from Afghanistan to Zimbabwe.

Gallup asked hundreds of questions about health, wealth, relationships, jobs and communities, and sampled attitudes to well-being among more than ninety percent of the world's population. They concluded that well-being embraces five broad areas of life. They don't include "every nuance of what's important in life but they do represent the five broad cadres that are essential to most people."

- <u>Career Well-being</u>: how you occupy your time or simply liking what you do every day
- <u>Social Well-being</u>: having strong relationships and love in your life
- <u>Financial Well-being</u>: effectively managing your economic life
- <u>Physical Well-being</u>: having good health and energy to get things done on a daily basis

- <u>Community Well-being</u>: your sense of engagement with the area where you live

Gallup concluded that while sixty-six percent of people are doing well in at least one of these areas, just seven percent are thriving in all five. In his book *Well-Being: The Five Essential Elements*, Tom Rath comments, "If we're struggling in any one of these domains, as most of us are, it damages our well-being and wears on our daily life. When we strengthen our well-being in any one of these areas we will have better days, months and decades. But we're not getting the most out of our lives unless we're living effectively in all five." Genuine, deep happiness and well-being come from having balance and fulfillment across each of these areas.

The Gallup research underlines the deep significance to your overall well-being of being in your Element in career well-being. Perhaps the most basic well-being question we can ask ourselves, says Rath, is "Do you like what you do each day?" At a fundamental level, says Rath, we all need something to do and ideally something to look forward to when we wake up every day. Yet only twenty percent of people in the Gallup study can give a strong yes in response.

"What you spend your time doing each day shapes your identity, whether you're a student, parent, volunteer, retiree or have a more conventional job. We spend the majority of our waking hours during the week doing something that we consider a career, occupation, vocation or job. When people first meet, they ask each other, 'What do you do?' If your answer to that question is something you find fulfilling and meaningful you're likely thriving in career well-being."

If you don't regularly do something you enjoy, even if it's not something you get paid to do, the odds of your having high well-being in other areas diminish rapidly. People with high career well-being are more than twice as likely to feel happy in their lives overall. "Imagine that you have great social relationships, financial security and good physical health," says Rath, "but you don't like what you do every day. Chances are, much of your social time is spent worrying or complaining about your lousy job. And this causes stress, taking a toll on your physical health. If your career well-being is low, it's easy to see how it can cause deterioration in other areas over time."

So how do you rate against these five areas of well-being? In Exercise Seven, you identified your own categories. With those still in mind, evaluate yourself now against the five I've just introduced.

Exercise Ten: Circles of Well-Being

- Look at each of the five areas of well-being. Would you add any others?
- Take a fresh piece of paper and draw a small circle in the middle with your name in the center. Draw five (or more) circles well spaced out around it: one for each of the main areas of well-being.
- Take each of them in turn and think about your own life and how you'd evaluate it in these terms. What words or images would you use to express your current experience or feelings in each of these areas of well-being? Put them in the circles.
- Take each circle in turn and do a few paragraphs of automatic writing. What issues and questions do they raise for you?

Assuming you have not given yourself a perfect score in all areas of well-being—and if you have, congratulations: you should write a book about it—how do you set about becoming happier overall and where does finding your Element fit in? The answer may be surprising.

Increasing Your Happiness

Throughout this book, we've talked about your life in terms of your biological inheritance, your actual circumstances, and how you act in the world. In *The How of Happiness,* Sonja Lyubomirsky also argues that there are three main factors that affect your levels of personal happiness: your circumstances, your biological disposition and your behavior. All three of these are significant in shaping your happiness. But one matters most.

CIRCUMSTANCES

Of all the factors that contribute to different levels of personal happiness, our actual circumstances—health, wealth, status and so on—contribute only about ten percent. A great deal of science supports this conclusion. For example, "the richest Americans, those earning more than $10 million annually, reported levels of personal happiness only slightly greater than the office staffs and blue-collar workers they employ." People who live in poverty or in challenging environments often report levels of happiness that differ little from those who live in affluent surroundings. As we noted earlier, happiness and well-being are based on many more factors than our material circumstances alone. A much more significant factor is our individual biological inheritance.

BIOLOGY

Our individual capacity for happiness is partly inherited. It is part of our biological makeup. Studies of identical and fraternal twins suggest that we're all born with a particular happiness set point that originates from our biological mother or father or both: "This is a baseline or potential for happiness to which we are bound to return even after major setbacks or triumphs," Lyubomirsky says. I'm sure you've seen the truth of this in your own life and among the people you know. Some people are naturally buoyant and cheerful, and others seem naturally long-suffering. Often their outlook has little to do with the events they're actually facing.

My own father, Jim, had a catastrophic accident when he was forty-five. He and my mother, Ethel, had seven children. In the late fifties, he'd been out of work for months during a dark period for the economy in Liverpool. Eventually, he found a job as a steel erector with a construction company. Within a few weeks of being back in work, a large wooden beam fell from high above him and broke his neck. For several days, it wasn't certain that he'd survive the accident. He did survive, but was a quadriplegic for the remaining eighteen years of his life, confined to a surgical bed and a wheelchair.

Before his accident, he was a man of great physical strength and tremendous character, very kind, caring and bitingly funny. Following the accident, we all lived in anxiety about the future. Although he never walked again or had the use of his hands, he did keep his character and his outlook. With my mother's love and support, he remained head of the family and a constant source of inspiration, wisdom and laughter to everyone who met him.

I know he had his dark days and in the immediate months after the accident he contemplated suicide, as many do who suffer sudden and devastating paralysis. Some succeed. Being completely paralyzed, he couldn't act on the impulse. Over the months and years his spirit returned to where it had been before the accident. In his last eighteen years, he had many wonderful times, enjoyed his life and enriched ours more than I can say.

One of the reasons my dad was able to recover his sense of perspective and to be as happy as he was for the rest of his life was my mum. She was just as remarkable as he was. She had tremendous energy and a huge appetite for people and life. She was also one of seven children, six girls and one boy in their case. She was born in 1919 in Liverpool, just after the First World War. Her father was a theatrical photographer. He was killed in a road accident when she was young, and her own mother raised the family in some hardship in the years between World Wars I and II. My memories of growing up myself among all of these aunts and uncles and numerous cousins in the Liverpool of the 1950s and 1960s are of tremendous kinship and the unabated hysteria of family gatherings. My mum had a great eye for design, loved the theater, fashion, movies and dancing. She loved to work with her hands and collected and decorated doll houses and miniatures and made rag dolls. For a while, the highlight of all family weddings and celebrations was a mass tap dance to "Lullaby of Broadway." She was always the first one up.

Whatever else was going on, she was always looking forward—to the next project, the next event, the next trip, the next get-together. She did all of this while taking care of seven children with no domestic appliances at all, with very little money when we were all young, and with my dad incapacitated for the last eighteen years of their marriage. They were also dealing with my illness when I was young and with all the other problems and ill-nesses that hit large families, wherever they are. But like his, her spirit was indomitable and her passion for life was vast. And they loved each other and being with each other. Their disposition guaranteed their happiness at some level, whatever else they had to deal with.

How much does your disposition influence your levels of personal happiness and well-being? Research suggests that it may account for up to fifty percent of how happy you are at any given time. So, if your biological disposition plays such a large part in your levels of happiness and there is not much you can do about that, and if your material circumstances have a relatively small role, what can you do to become happier? The good news is, quite a lot. Whatever your disposition and circumstances, you have more power than you might imagine to increase your own levels of happiness and well-being.

BEHAVIOR

Research suggests that 40 percent of what affects your actual levels of happiness is what you choose to do and how you choose to think and feel: in other words, your own behavior. The key to happiness lies not in changing your genetic makeup, which you can't, or your circumstances, which may or may not be possible, but in your "daily intentional activities." Finding and being in your Element is a critical part of that process.

French Buddhist monk Matthieu Ricard is an accomplished writer, the subject of a study on happiness conducted at the University of Wisconsin-Madison, and someone dubbed in media circles as "the happiest man in the world." In *Happiness: A Guide to Developing Life's Most Important Skill*, Ricard notes that people often equate happiness with trivial things, "such as that of one French actress: 'For me, happiness is eating a tasty plate of spaghetti,' or 'Walking in the snow under the stars' and so on. The many definitions of happiness that I encountered contradicted one another and often seemed vague or superficial. So in the light of the analytical and contemplative science of mind that I had encountered through the kindness of teachers, I embarked on trying to unravel the meaning and mechanism of genuine happiness, and of course suffering."

He states that he has "come to understand that although some people are naturally happier than others, their happiness is still vulnerable and incomplete, and that achieving durable happiness as a way of being is a skill. It requires sustained effort in training the mind and developing a set of human qualities, such as inner peace, mindfulness and altruistic love."

Projecting Happiness

A few years back, writer Gretchen Rubin decided to embark on a campaign to make herself happier, even though she acknowledges (and assured her husband) that she was already relatively happy. She chronicled her journey in *The Happiness Project*. The subtitle here speaks volumes (or at least one volume): *Or, Why I Spent a Year Trying to Sing in the Morning, Clean My Closets, Fight Right, Read Aristotle, and Generally Have More Fun*. She decided to focus on boosting her happiness in different parts of her life, such as marriage, work, play and money. She chose to boost one part per month, for a year.

"Contemporary research shows that happy people are more

altruistic, more productive, more helpful, more likable, more creative, more resilient, more interested in others, friendlier, and healthier," she says. "Happy people make better friends, colleagues, and citizens. I wanted to be one of those people." On her Happiness Project website, she lists Four Splendid Truths. The fourth, and most salient of these in my opinion, is "You're not happy unless you think you're happy. Corollary: You're happy if you think you're happy."

When all of the authors I've mentioned speak about true and deep happiness, they are often speaking in their own ways about finding your Element. This is what Andrew Weil is writing about when he mentions "knowing that I was the person I was supposed to be." It's a function of the "sustained effort" that Ricard identifies. It's at the heart of so much of Rubin's Happiness Project, and Lyubomirsky's "intentional activities," and Rath's and Seligman's views on well-being.

The combination of happiness and meaning propels the life you are living to something that seems far more like play than like work.

Getting Over Yourself

While happiness is an internal state, it is often enhanced by looking beyond yourself and engaging with the needs of others. Dean Cycon's heart has gone out to the disadvantaged since he was very young. "My first big underdog crush was on the New York Mets growing up," he told me. "When I was ten, the Mets were formed and they lost their first ten games. The team was full of leftover should-have-been-retired baseball players who couldn't make it anymore but were really trying hard. I was just struck with their desire to go someplace, and was swept away with the excitement of the underdog."

Dean spent many of his schoolboy days sticking up for kids who were being picked on by bullies. Even though he wasn't very big himself, he felt a strong need to fight—literally—for the downtrodden. By the time he was a teen, he already had a strong sense that you could make the right thing happen if you pushed hard enough for it. However, a broadcast he saw when he was in high school drove the message home to him in the most meaningful way.

"I was watching the news, and President Johnson came on to announce the suspension of bombing of North Vietnam. I realized right then that the only reason he did that was because people were in the streets expressing their outrage over America's involvement in Vietnam, and at the head of those people were social justice lawyers, William Kunstler in particular. That's when I said, 'That's what I want to do.'"

Dean became a lawyer, realizing while he was in college that he was particularly interested in the struggles Native Americans were having to retain their land and their culture. While doing other sorts of legal work to pay the bills, he spent as much time as he could defending Native Americans, and this caused his reputation to grow. "Word got out on the 'tom-tom telephone' that there was a young lawyer who was willing to help native peoples in their struggles against governments and big companies. I started to get calls around the United States, then around Canada, and then overseas. I started working with indigenous peoples in Latin America. That led to my giving lectures in colleges about indigenous peoples' problems and about environmental issues in the forests around the world."

One such lecture—about the farmers of Brazil—took place at the University of Rhode Island. After the talk, a professor approached Dean to tell him about a friend who had a coffee shop in Providence. The friend bought coffee from Brazil, but he knew that the farmers who grew the coffee were getting very little of this money and were living in poverty. The friend wanted to help the farmers, but he didn't know how, and the professor thought a conversation with Dean might be beneficial.

"I realized that helping this man was a furtherance of the passion that I had. In 1998, we formed Coffee Kids, the world's first nonprofit organization to work in the coffee lands. My job was to go into those villages, meet with the farmers, and create programs that would address some of their biggest issues, whether it was water, or school, or income generation. The other guy would go to coffee companies around the country and get them to give us money to fund it. It was great work, but after a number of years, I realized something was bothering me. We were doing this great work for the farmers, but the coffee companies were only giving a few thousand dollars to do these projects. They weren't changing the way they were behaving in the villages, so the cycle of poverty wasn't being broken. Still, the companies were advertising to their customers as though they were really engaged in making change in the world. I wondered what it would look like if a company really paid good money for the coffee to the farmers."

By this point, Dean already knew that he no longer had any interest in continuing to be a lawyer. Too much about the day-to-day of the legal profession didn't seem to mesh with who he was. However, he also knew that he needed to do something bigger and with larger social implications than Coffee Kids. Thinking of the coffee farmers, he wondered, "What would it look like if a company engaged in the big issues of the day in the villages, and took a sense of responsibility for what was going on in those villages where they were buying their product so cheaply? Would it be possible for a company to do both of those things and be profitable? If that were possible, then I would have created a new model that showed you could be a sensitive caring businessperson and still be profitable. That's when Dean's Beans was born in 1993."

Eighteen years later, Dean's Beans is a thriving operation selling its coffee online, at retail and in coffee bars. The company works directly with coffee farmers in fourteen countries, setting up equitable development programs with all of them. For Dean, this is a tremendously hands-on process. He establishes these programs himself, traveling all over the world to do so.

"If I were a timid person, I couldn't do this because I go to places that are sometimes physically dangerous, certainly challenging to one's health, and are cultures that can be quite different from ours. I love adventure, I love to travel, I love different cultures, and I love to explore. So yes, it's social justice, but it's absolutely perfect for my personality. I get comments from people all the time saying, 'Wow, I could never go to Ethiopia and live in those villages,' or 'I could never go to Papua New Guinea and get naked in front of seven thousand people,' but I love it. It's so much about what you can and can't do in the world. I really admire lawyers who can argue in court and write briefs, but I can't do that; that's why I left the law. I can't sit in an office, and I can't write papers."

The success of Dean's business model has proven that profit and social conscience are fully compatible. These days, when he's not helping land reclamation efforts in Sumatra or developing carbon-neutral coffee in Peru, Dean speaks to audiences about applying his model to their businesses. "I love to get people excited about what I'm excited about," he told me, "and I have a talent for it."

Working with others, helping them boost themselves up, and raising as much awareness as he can makes Dean Cycon happy. He couldn't do anything to help the '62 Mets, but he's made considerably more of an impact ever since.

Like Dean Cycon, Craig Kielburger has a strong sense of purpose, and this drove him to do something very few preteens ever consider doing. On a morning in 1995, Kielburger was looking for the comics pages in the *Toronto Star* when he came across a headline that read, "Battled Child Labor, Boy, 12, Murdered." The article told the story of a Pakistani boy named Iqbal Masih who had been sold into slavery at age four and had become an increasingly influential voice in revealing the miserable conditions of people like him and in fighting for the rights of children. His efforts led to his assassination, and Kielburger—the same age as the slain boy—found himself moved by this in a way that nothing had moved him before. He decided to learn as much as he could about human rights, even convincing his parents to let him travel to Southeast Asia with a Canadian rights activist. Seeing child laborers working under deplorable conditions changed his life and gave him his purpose. When he returned home, he rallied a group of his fellow seventh graders to fight for children's rights throughout the world. "It wasn't anything dramatic," Kielburger said of the initial effort. "We passed around a couple of petitions to political leaders and heads of corporations. Then, a few of us gave speeches in schools and for religious and community groups, and it just began to snowball from there."

The organization those kids started in that Thornhill, Ontario, school became Free the Children, the largest network of children helping children in the world. The organization has launched education and development programs in forty-five countries with a stated purpose: "Free the children from poverty. Free the children from exploitation. Free the children from the notion that they are powerless to effect change."

More than a hundred thousand youths are involved in Free the Children today. They have raised the money to build hundreds of schools in developing nations, send millions of dollars in medical aid and develop programs to offer alternatives that allow children in these countries to become something other than child laborers and child soldiers.

Kielburger faced enormous challenges in his attempt to put together Free the Children, but his sense of purpose wouldn't allow him to relent. "While Free the Children was founded on the basis of ending child exploitation and poverty," he said during an interview, "the greatest challenge was in proving that young people were not apathetic and indifferent, but important change makers. At Free the Children, we made it our task to show the world that young people were in fact resourceful, creative and insightful, and had an uncanny ability to channel hopelessness and frustration into positive action. Who could understand young people's issues better than young people themselves?"

"The night before I came home from Southeast Asia," he said to a reporter, speaking of his first trip abroad, "a radio talk-show host in Toronto announced that at my age, I should be interested in girls, sex and video games—certainly not child labor. It's astounding how so many people share that definition of a 'normal' child. They limit the spirit and enthusiasm of children. In fact, I met with drug dealers who have greater faith in children to run drugs than

I see people in the United States and Canada put in their own kids."

Kielburger has become an important voice not only for his own causes, but for activism of all stripes. Clearly someone who understands the importance of doing something meaningful for one's personal satisfaction, he advocates that teens get involved in causes that resonate with them as early as possible. He's even put together a seven-step plan for kids to embark on their own social missions:

1. Find your passion: choose your issue
2. Research the reality
3. Build your "dream team"
4. Meet around the round table
5. Set your mission: set your goals!
6. Take action!
7. Bring in the FUNK!

I think we can all attest to the value of bringing in the funk, and while I never would have phrased it that way myself, I couldn't have said it any better.

Being in your Element is a powerful way of increasing your happiness and sense of well-being, but it doesn't guarantee that you'll be happy all the time. People in their Element still have bad days. They still suffer annoying friends and colleagues. They still face times when everything seems to be going wrong, and they still need to muddle through stretches of too little sleep and too much stress. I believe two things to be very true, though. One is that being in your Element dramatically increases the odds of your being happy more often. The other is that feeling a strong sense of happiness while doing something is a good sign that what you're doing might be your Element.

Some more questions to ponder:

- How does your sense of well-being compare with other times in your life?
- When do you feel at your happiest?
- Do you feel that what you spend most of your time doing has a real purpose, for you or for others?
- Do you find that purpose personally rewarding? In what ways?
- What would you think of as success in your life?
- Which causes inspire you?
- What would you include in your own "happiness project"?

CHAPTER SIX

What's Your Attitude?

T O B E I N your Element you have to be willing to do what it takes. Finding your Element is not only about aptitude and passion. It's about attitude. In chapter four, I connected being in your Element with positive rather than negative feelings and said that these are strongly associated with a sense of real happiness. In chapter five, I suggested that the two major factors in being happy are your natural disposition and your actual behavior. In this chapter, we look at how your own attitudes may be helping or hindering you in finding your Element and at how they relate to your general temperament, disposition and type of personality.

By now, you may be closer to understanding your own aptitudes and you may have a clearer sense of what you love to do. If so, that's great. If not, don't worry. This is a process, not a test, and if you persist, you will get closer to what you're looking for. Everything depends on how much this matters to you and on how determined you are in your quest. If you know what your Element is, you need the self-belief and determination to pursue it. If you don't know what it is, you need to feel entitled to look for it.

Along the way, you'll almost certainly encounter obstacles.

Some may be in the world around you. You may be limited by circumstances, culture, by work or the lack of it, by the attitudes of family or friends or by financial pressures. I'll come back to these in the next chapter. But some obstacles may lie within you. You may be too comfortable in your current way of living to want to take a risk. You may prefer the life you know, even if you don't enjoy it, to the uncertain prospects of trying to change it. You may be held back by self-doubt, or lack of belief. To find your Element you need to ask what and where the real obstacles are.

How Full Is Your Glass?

In *The Element*, we quoted the following lines from Shakespeare's *Hamlet*: "There is nothing either good or bad but thinking makes it so." There is a fundamental truth in this. I said earlier that we don't see the world or ourselves directly but through veils of ideas, feelings and values. Some of these we learn through the cultures we live in, some through our unique experiences in life, and some through our own personalities. Just as one person may love to do something that someone else would loathe, we all see the world through different filters.

Throughout this book, I've resisted suggesting or endorsing simple categories of people into which you might try to fit yourself. As individuals we are all infinitely complex and we change, too, over time and in the light of our personal experiences. Of all the areas we've looked at—aptitudes, learning styles and passion— none is more complex than disposition and attitude. So you have to do some work here.

Exercise 11: How Do You See Things?

In this chapter, I'm going to offer some working definitions of terms, including personality, temperament, disposition and attitude. We'll also review various attempts to categorize people into "types." As you read through the chapter:

- Ask yourself critically if these make sense to you and if and how they apply to you. Do you feel that any of them properly describes you?
- As you do this, keep a notebook and write down key words (not sentences) that you feel describe your outlook on the world, and those that, for now at least, definitely don't.
- Do you see any patterns or connections in them? Using four different colors, circle each word according to whether you see these characteristics as:

  Positive
  Negative
  Moving you forward
  Holding you back.

- Look at the whole list and how you've colored it in. Do you think this is a fair profile of your outlook at the moment? Do you see any need and room for change and development?
- When you've finished the chapter, do a quick Internet search on "attitude tests." You'll find there are a lot of them. I've suggested a few to start with in the notes to

this chapter at the end of the book. Try a few and compare the results.

Before we get to ways of thinking about attitude, here's an example of how big a difference attitude can make.

Seeing Through the Barriers

Some people find their Element easily and without resistance. Others have to push hard against the attitudes of other people and sometimes against their own. Take Jef Lynch, for example. On the basis of the job description, he shouldn't have even bothered going in for the interview when he learned that General Motors was looking for a training van instructor for their Chevrolet Motor Division, a job that Jef wanted more than anything. The job required a college degree, and Jef had never spent a day in college. It also required him to buy a suit and a pair of dress shoes for the interview and to try to do something to clean up his hands that, according to Jef, looked like "creature hands" from all of his work as a mechanic at a local Chevrolet dealership. In all, the opportunity didn't seem promising.

He got the job anyway. Like my brother Derek, Jef had a passion for cars. "I had been disassembling and reassembling everything I could get my hands on since the time I could walk," he told me. He also has an uncompromising commitment to excellence in what he does, which came across so loudly that the GM executive who interviewed him overlooked his lack of formal education. Still, once he had the position, Jef had to deal with the reality that he was in an entirely new environment that he'd never been in before.

"I got the job and my whole life changed. Within a week, I was flying out to St. Louis to learn how to be a Chevrolet training van instructor. I'd never been in a plane before. I'd never been out of the area before. I was so intimidated that by the end of the week, I was going to drive the car over, put it in the parking lot and just walk home. But when I got home I realized, 'Wow, I did it.' Nobody knew how scared I was."

Jef excelled at the position, but that didn't mean he'd stopped running up against brick walls. A promotion to service rep created a new kind of barrier for him. "It was a pretty important job because you had to go in and authorize millions of dollars' worth of repairs a year and help them with customer service. I hated it because when you're in the position of holding the purse strings, everybody wants money and they're going to lie to you all the time. It was just not good for me. This friend of mine worked at the General Motors Training Center in Dedham, Massachusetts. I grew up in Dedham and all my life I'd driven by there wondering what it was all about. I told my boss at Chevrolet that I appreciated what he'd done for me but that I hated my job and that I thought I could do something with the training center. He helped and I got an interview."

The next barrier for Jef was his age. He was much younger than the other instructors in a field where management was convinced that experience mattered. Still, they gave Jef a shot, making him the youngest instructor in training center history at the time, and the only one without a college degree. "Luck and opportunity have a lot to do with it," he told me, but what he said immediately after might have been more revealing. "The key is paying attention when the opportunity is there and not just walking by it."

For Jef, life kept putting up stop signs, and Jef, a committed street racer in his youth, kept driving right through them. His new position required him to translate what the engineers were passing along—and in an increasingly computerized world, this was akin to learning Mandarin—to help the mechanics do their jobs. Rather than being cowed by this, Jef used his innate understanding of cars and his very recent experience as a line mechanic to interpret the information in ways that more experienced instructors couldn't.

"I started taking materials and rewriting them, making my own handouts. Everybody started using them, so I started writing materials for the training center. I guess they figured it was easier to have me do it than fight with me. I ended up writing a bunch of books that I printed locally and people were buying like crazy. I ended up taking three of my books and turning it into one book that sold all over the world.

"When all the computer stuff came out with cars, I totally understood it. They had us looking at computer data coming out on a handheld scanner. The scanner would get updated so infrequently that you could have all kinds of intermittent problems that blew right by it. I decided that I needed to have a real good lab scope. In Burlington, Massachusetts, there was an outlet for Tektronix. Scopes are big money, so I walked in the front door and I introduced myself. I told them what I wanted to do, and the manager came over and I explained to him what I needed. He brought me over to a tech guy and the tech guy got involved with the service manager, and the next thing I know, they have the people in the home office on the phone.

"I wound up getting equipment for free because I talked to them in an intelligent fashion, I'm not sounding like a smart ass, and now I've also made them see that there's an opportunity to sell this equipment in a fashion they've never dreamed of before. I ended up with a Tektronix rep traveling with me for two weeks around the United States showing people how to use scopes while they provided the scopes for free. I also got a job writing a book about using the scope that Tektronix paid me for. That spilled over into other business. I ended up giving speeches at colleges and vocational schools. I've been on the board of a couple of training schools."

That's quite a leap for someone who was once so intimidated by his lack of qualifications that he nearly walked out on his first real opportunity. What Jef Lynch learned relatively early in life is that the things that are stopping you often exist only in your mind. "I don't see the barriers that other people see. With Tektronix, I just walked in the door and started talking to people. Everything I do, I do like that."

Jef is retired now, though that's hardly stopped him from climbing over walls. He runs a company that builds and services high-performance cars, and in his spare time, he's designing a revolutionary new engine. I assume he'll be as successful at these pursuits as he's been in every other because Jef has always understood at a fundamental level where he was and where he wanted to go.

Jef's story is a powerful illustration that attitude can be everything in finding your Element. He has a natural aptitude for what he does and he loves it, too. But others may have been put off by not having conventional qualifications and not feeling entitled to the promotions he wanted. Jef wasn't. As he says, he doesn't see the barriers that other people see. His story offers elegant proof that sometimes if you don't see barriers, they're not really there.

Who Are You?

In chapter four I made a general distinction between mind, consciousness and personality and said that by "personality" I mean your general outlook and disposition to yourself and to the world around you. There are of course many facets of personality. Let me briefly elaborate on three that are especially important here: your temperament, disposition and character. Like the various words for love, these three terms are often used in overlapping ways and even as synonyms, but each of them points to different aspects of personality.

By temperament, I mean your typical patterns of behaviors, feelings and responses. Your natural temperament affects how you see the world, how you act in it, and what attracts your interests and excites your passions. This is what we imply when we say that some people have an artistic, a scientific or a religious temperament and so on.

By disposition, I mean your customary moods and attitudes: whether you are naturally cheerful, for example, or cynical, optimistic or pessimistic; whether you typically think that your glass is half empty or half full.

By character, I mean your overall moral qualities, including honesty, loyalty, courage, determination, and their opposites and variations.

Your biological inheritance affects your levels of happiness because it influences your temperament, disposition and character. But it doesn't determine them. One way of distinguishing temperament and disposition is to say that your temperament is what you were born with, while your disposition evolves through your experiences in the world. Although some features of your temperament are relatively unchanging, your disposition will almost certainly change as your experiences increase and you mature. This is especially true of your attitudes to yourself and to what you're capable of achieving.

Temperament and disposition are your general orientation to the world. Attitudes are an expression of your temperament and disposition, but they are more specific. A physical attitude is a stance we take to do something practical: serving a tennis ball, lifting a weight, preparing to run or bracing for trouble. A mental attitude is also a position we take, to a situation, an issue or a relationship, for example.

An attitude is a point of view. In geometry, an attitude is an angle of inclination. In your consciousness, too, your attitude is the angle or perspective from which you perceive something. Two people watching the same situation may see it completely differently, as any trial lawyer will tell you. They may literally see it from different physical positions, which affect what they see. They may also see it from the same physical position but through completely different "points of view."

The good news is that like your general disposition, your particular attitudes can change too. New ideas and information, fresh insights and experiences can reframe how you see things. Whether you see the cup half empty or half full is often a matter of choice and experience. It can have critical bearing on whether and how you find your Element. Take the story of Sue Kent, for example.

Best Foot Forward

Sue Kent lives in Swansea in Wales, and is a qualified masseuse. In 2012, she was an official masseuse for the British Paralympics team in London. She has her own practice in London and

Swansea and she trains other people in her techniques. What makes her achievements so remarkable is that Sue was born with severely underdeveloped arms. Her arms are just eight inches long, and she has only seven fingers. She can't give massages with her hands; instead she gives them with her feet. Her clients lie on the floor and she massages them as she sits on a bench above them.

Sue's arms didn't develop normally because her mother had been prescribed the drug Thalidomide when she was pregnant. For several years in the 1970s, Thalidomide was widely prescribed to help relieve morning sickness. It was then found to interfere with the normal development of the fetus and caused numerous birth defects. Amid huge legal and medical controversy, Thalidomide was eventually withdrawn from use. More than ten thousand babies were affected, many of whom were born with severe physical disabilities, including Sue.

Now fifty, Sue has always been determined to overcome the many challenges that she has faced from childhood. Over the years, she's been actively involved in swimming, horse riding, surfing and ballet. "I've always worked out of my own way of doing things," she says. The more people see this disability, "the more normal it becomes and the less people will be stupid about it."

She married and now has children of her own. When she left the "sheltered world" of bringing up her children, she decided she had to continue to challenge herself and other people. She worked for a time in marketing and advertising, but had to give that up to take care of her parents when they became ill. During her time back at home, her son strained his back sailing. She started to massage him to relieve the pain. It worked so well and she enjoyed it so much that she began to wonder if she could do it for a living. Eventually, she applied to the University of Wales to take a certified training program in sports massage. Some of her tutors were skeptical that she'd be able to succeed using only her feet. It was certainly hard work, and took her more than a year to develop her own techniques and to condition her leg and foot muscles to do this effectively.

Most people's feet harden through everyday use. Sue's have to be supple and sensitive. After a series of pedicures and conditioning treatments, she found a further solution. She commissioned a glove manufacturer to make her some soft rubber foot gloves to protect her feet while she's "walking around during the day and doing all my other jobs."

Sue proved her doubters wrong and set up her own company, Enjoy Feet. So far she's the only sports massage therapist in the UK who's qualified to treat clients in this way. "The majority of people I've treated are curious at first, but then they say it feels like a really big hand and that it's better because you're covering more surface area. Stretching is fun because I have to place peoples' feet under my armpits. I treat a lot of men and have had weightlifters because I can give them a very firm massage. Because I've got such strength in my legs, it doesn't take too much effort to really get in and sort those muscles out."

Sue was appointed to the Paralympics team after three years' practice as a professional therapist. This was a passionate, personal goal. "I wanted to see if I could be involved in sport in some way at a high level," she said. "For the guys at the Paralympics to be doing what they're doing is phenomenal. I couldn't wait to be part of it." She also wanted to challenge the stereotypes that confront people with disabilities. "I hope I inspire other disabled people and show them that they don't need to do a job that's just about sitting behind a desk with a computer."

Sue Kent is a striking example of what Carol Dweck would call the "growth mindset."

Changing Your Mindset

Carol Dweck is a psychologist at Stanford University in California. For more than twenty years, her research has focused on how people's dispositions and attitudes affect what they achieve. "The view you adopt of yourself," she says, "can determine whether you become the person you want to be and whether you accomplish the things you value." In her book *Mindset*, Dweck describes two radically different sets of attitudes, which she calls fixed and growth mindsets.

People with a fixed mindset tend to believe that personal qualities like intelligence and talent are set at birth and cannot be changed. They are simply "carved in stone." A fixed mindset often "creates an urgency to prove yourself over and over." If you believe you only have a certain amount of intelligence, certain personality and certain moral character, "well then you'd better prove that you have a healthy dose of them. It simply wouldn't look right to look or feel deficient in these most basic characteristics."

The fixed mindset is constantly reinforced, says Dweck, by some forms of education and also by popular images of IQ tests that give set numbers for qualities like intelligence. Very many people with fixed mindsets are obsessed with "one consuming goal of proving themselves" in the classroom, in their careers and in their relationships. Will I succeed or fail? Will I look smart or dumb? Will I be accepted or rejected? Will I feel like a winner or loser? People with a fixed mindset tend to think that aptitudes and disposition are "simply a hand you're dealt and have to live with." If you believe that, you may find yourself "always trying to convince yourself and others that you have a royal flush when you're secretly worried it's a pair of tens."

The growth mindset is wholly different. It is based on the belief that you can develop your aptitudes and possibilities through your own efforts. Although people differ in their biological inheritance, those with the growth mindset believe that "everyone can change and grow through application and experience."

One of the oldest debates in human development is about the relationship between nature and nurture. Are your capabilities and achievements shaped more by biology or by experience? The dominant scientific and philosophical view now is that there is a dynamic relation between nature and nurture. Each deeply affects the other. Like the rest of your body, your brain continues to evolve during your life as new experiences and skills generate new neural pathways and networks.

Carol Dweck's approach is based on this principle of growth and evolution. As she puts it, "each person has a unique genetic endowment. People may start with different temperaments and different attitudes, but it's clear that experiences, training and personal effort take them the rest of the way." The growth mindset is rooted in the view that it is impossible to know what people are really capable of achieving unless they apply themselves in the right way, with the right effort and commitment. "The passion for stretching yourself and sticking to it even, or especially, when it's not going well is the hallmark of the growth mindset."

Let me give you one more example of how the growth mindset enabled someone to find her Element against every sort of obstacle.

I said in chapter three that if you live far from the ocean and have never set foot on a boat, you'd never know if you had a gift for sailing. That's true, unless you're Ellen MacArthur. Ellen has had an unusual journey, in every sense of the word. At the age of twenty-two, she was the fastest person ever to sail solo, nonstop around the world. She could not have had a less likely starting point for a career at sea. She was born far from the ocean in a low-income community in England and could not have been further away from having a life as a competitive sailor. But from a young age, Ellen was haunted by the ocean and determined to sail it.

"Sailing around the world had been a dream for me from the moment I first sailed when I was four years old," she told me. "My Auntie Thea had bought a boat that she worked on for two years before it was ready to sail, and my Nan took my elder brother and I down to the South East coast to sail for a few days. I remember vividly the excitement of seeing the boat for the first time, and when I scrambled onboard and peered down into her tiny cabin, I saw a miniature house. But the moment I still remember, like it was yesterday, was when we hoisted the sails for the first time. As the boat came alive I felt the greatest sense of freedom I had ever experienced. As a child who had grown up in far inland in Derbyshire, this was quite overwhelming.

"From that moment on, sailing took over my life, despite having no sailing friends to share my passion with. My schools were all in a coal-mining town, which had very little mining left, and reaching for the stars was not something that was encouraged. If I'd said that my dream was to sail around the world I think everyone would have thought I was bonkers. So I kept it for me."

While still in school, Ellen began saving birthday and Christmas money to buy a boat, finally cobbling together enough money to do exactly that. Still, she felt the need to put her sailing dreams on hold in an attempt to get a university education. She considered studying to become a vet, but poor test grades and a bout of glandular fever made college a remote possibility. She now considers this setback to be "the best thing that could have happened to me."

"One morning at two o'clock on my third week of being ill, there was a program on the TV about the Whitbread Round the World Race. As the minutes unfolded, my dream of sailing around the world suddenly seemed achievable. The images of the sailors in that race flicked across the screen and I suddenly realized that I could sail around the world without having to buy a boat. I could go out and find a sponsor.

"One week later I was out of bed, and two months later I was sleeping on the floor of a nautical school in Hull on the east coast of England learning how to teach sailing and navigation. I was up late every night learning the lights on their computer program, or wandering down the banks of the river identifying ships. Twelve months later I left that same port on my first singlehanded voyage to sail around Britain. That was in 1995. I was eighteen years old and as I sailed down the river alone at the beginning of a four-and-a-half-month journey, I felt that my future was unfolding!"

Within the year, Ellen had crossed the Atlantic twice, and in the two following years, she made three more crossings, including two entirely by herself. She looked for sponsors, which was a challenge because she wasn't well known in the sailing community, but by the time she was twenty-two, she'd landed a sponsorship from Kingfisher PLC to sail around the world.

"At sea I was in my element. Processing data from a million sources, and outputting that data into speed, whilst at the same time not making a mistake that could end my life there and then. The first time I sailed my yacht *Kingfisher*, I honestly thought I was in heaven. I was so happy I sailed her half way around the world in training and then two weeks later won my first race in her against the best solo sailors in the world. Later that year, I set off for the Vendee Globe, the solo non-stop around-the-world race, in which I finished second. Four years later, after building a seventy-five-foot trimaran, I became the fastest person ever to sail solo nonstop around the world. I was doing my dream job and living my dream life. I knew then that anything is possible."

Finding your Element depends on discovering your aptitudes and passions. Ellen discovered hers at an early stage and in very unlikely circumstances. But, like Sue, to actually be in her Element, she had to test her own boundaries and believe strongly enough in her own possibilities. For them and for you, it's a matter of attitude and of personality.

Classifying Personality

So what sort of personality are you? The fact is that our individual personalities are as different from each other as our physical appearances. Just as cultures have different concepts of love, there have been various attempts to classify types of personality. They range from the scientific to the metaphysical and the occult. None of these is universally accepted for the good reason that human beings are infinitely variable. But it may be helpful to think about your own temperament, disposition and attitudes in relation to these different conceptions of personality types.

One of the earliest systems for classifying personality was developed in the first millennium BC by astrologers in what's now known as the Middle East. I won't dwell here on the details of these astrological types because they're so well known. The rationale for them is interesting, though. They're based on the four elements of water, earth, air and fire. Each of these is associated with three signs of the zodiac:

- Water: Pisces, Cancer and Scorpio
- Air: Aquarius, Gemini and Libra
- Earth: Capricorn, Taurus and Virgo
- Fire: Aries, Leo and Sagittarius.

According to astrology, you have the personality of whichever star sign you're born under. Interestingly, if you have an interest in stereotypes, the air and fire signs are sometimes said to be positive, extroverted and masculine; the water and earth signs are negative, introverted and feminine.

Star signs continue to influence how many people think of their personalities and their "fate" in life. Astrologers still predict life events based on their readings of astrological charts. There are good reasons to be skeptical of these claims, as I mentioned in the introduction when I commented on the Forer Effect. My father was a lifelong skeptic of star signs and astrological predictions. Mind you, I always liked to tell him that he wouldn't take these things seriously because he was a Virgo and Virgos don't believe in them.

A Sense of Humor

Another system that's nearly as ancient as star signs, but largely abandoned now, is the vaguely unpleasant bodily humors theory of personality. Even so, you may still recognize yourself in here somewhere. The Greek physician Hippocrates (460 to 370 BC) believed that personality was affected by bodily fluids, or humors: blood, yellow bile, black bile and phlegm. (I told you this wasn't pleasant.) Five hundred years later the Roman physician Galen (AD 131 to 200) took the theory of humors and combined it with the four elements to suggest various types of temperament:

sanguine, choleric, melancholic and phlegmatic. Each of these types was thought to be the result of too much of the humor in question.

Sanguine people love to socialize and tend to be outgoing, charismatic and socially confident. They can also be sensitive, compassionate, thoughtful, and need time to themselves.

Choleric people are ambitious and always happy to take the lead. They can be very passionate and energetic and can easily overwhelm people of other temperaments. They tend to be extreme in their approach to life and are also prone to swing between high enthusiasm and low depression.

The melancholic is essentially introverted and thoughtful. Melancholics are considerate of other people's feelings and can be overly sensitive to life's tragedies and crises. Melancholics are often involved in the arts, especially as writers and painters. They prefer to work alone and can sometimes become almost reclusive.

The phlegmatic is relaxed and quiet and tends to be kind to others and generally happy and content. They are slow to adapt to change. They like routine and being among familiar people, places and things. They are persistent and methodical and like to do a good job and see it through to the end.

In various forms, the concept of humors dominated thinking about personality types until the rise of modern science in the eighteenth and nineteenth centuries. As psychology developed as a discipline, new attempts were made to classify the innumerable ways in which individuals behave and relate to each other.

Inside Out

In 1921, Carl Jung published *Psychological Types*. It had a major impact on psychology and in popular culture and is still one of the most influential theories of personality. Jung's work was based on more than twenty years of study in psychology. His focus was not so much on classifying patterns of behavior as on understanding how people typically related to the world. It was Jung who developed the idea of introverts and extroverts that's become so much a part of modern conversation.

According to Jung, introversion and extroversion are modes of attention and engagement. The introvert is more oriented to the inner world, the extrovert more toward the outer world. Introversion is normally characterized by "a hesitant, reflective, retiring nature that keeps itself to itself"; extroversion by "an outgoing candid and accommodating nature that adapts easily to a given situation, quickly forms attachments and setting aside possible misgivings will often venture forth with careless confidence into unknown situations." As detached as he aimed to be, it's easy to get the impression that Jung was not terribly fond of extroverts. He did say, though, that no one is only introverted or extroverted. "Although each of us in the process of following our dominant inclination invariably depends on one attitude more than the other, the opposite attitude is still potentially there."

In addition to these two attitudes, Jung identifies four modes of orientation:

- Thinking—the process of conscious thought
- Sensation—perceiving the world through the physical senses

- Feeling—the process of subjective evaluation
- Intuition—the process of unconscious perception

He combined these two attitudes and four modes to suggest eight main personality types. He was careful to say that his classification system did not explain everything about individual psychological differences. Nor did he intend it as a way of labeling people. He saw it primarily as a tool for understanding similarities and differences among people often for the purposes of analysis and treatment. Neither did he have in mind a widespread scheme of practical application.

Nonetheless, Jung's system has been used as the basis of various approaches to classifying personality types that are used in business, education, coaching and career counseling. The best known of these is the Myers-Briggs personality type indicator (MBTI). The system was developed in the forties from Jung's writings by Catherine Cook Briggs and her daughter Isabel Briggs Myers. MBTI takes Jung's theory and combines the concepts of attributes and preferences to generate sixteen personality types. The MBTI testing system is designed to help you discover your own type by assessing yourself across four dimensions:

- Extroversion (E)—Introversion (I)
- Sensing (S)—Intuition (N)
- Thinking (T)—Feeling (F)
- Judging (J)—Perceiving (P)

The results generate one of sixteen four-letter codes, which is your personality type. (If you're interested, I came out as INFP). MBTI claims that the sixteen personality types cover everyone, at least broadly enough to be useful and reliable. This is not to say the people are not all unique. "A hundred people of the same personality types in the room would all be different because they have different parents, genes, experiences, interests and so on. But they would also have a tremendous amount in common."

MBTI is based on the assumption that your life and career choices should be based on a proper understanding of your abilities, interests and values. These are sometimes called "the big three" by MBTI practitioners. These characteristics may all evolve over time. As you gain work experience, you gain new skills, "as you live longer, you may pick up new interests and discard old ones. Often your goals in life are different later than they were earlier." Your type does not determine ability or predict success but it is intended "to help others discover what best motivates and energizes each of us as individuals and empowers us to seek these elements in the work that we choose to do."

I argued in *The Element* that all systems of classification have deficiencies, including MBTI. You should approach them all critically and not try to bend yourself to fit them. If you treat them as ways of generating questions and ideas about yourself, they can be useful. If you use them to brand and limit yourself, they are not.

A Question of Temperament

In this spirit, I find the next classification system particularly interesting. It's based on long-term studies of children and parents. Since we've all been children and had parents of one sort or another, it's a framework we can all use. I like it because it doesn't suggest a set number of personality types: it suggests dimensions of personality, which combine in many different ways in each of us.

Dr. Alex Thomas and Dr. Stella Chess were a husband and wife team of psychiatrists based in New York City. They had a particular interest in the idea of temperament, which they define in a way that relates to aptitude and passion as I use the terms here. Temperament, they say, has to be distinguished from two other qualities in individuals:

- What you can do—your abilities and talents
- Why you do it—your motivations and purposes
- Temperament—your styles of behavior

Through long-term studies of children's behavior, Chess and Thomas identified nine behavioral attributes and suggested that all children (and adults too) differ on each of these traits on a range from low to high. You might apply these to yourself and to people you know.

Sensitivity refers to how much stimulus a child needs to provoke a response. Is the child bothered by external stimuli like noises, textures or lights, or does the child seem to ignore them? "Some children," says Dr. Chess, "will blink at sunlight and some will scream. Some will scarcely notice a loud noise and some will be exquisitely sensitive to it."

Intensity refers to the energy level of a child's response. "A highly intense child may laugh out loud and shout; the low intensity child may have a quiet smile. In a negative mood, the high intensity child will scream and cry loudly; the low intensity child may whimper and have a mild fuss."

Activity refers to the child's physical energy. "A low activity child may watch TV quietly for hours. A high activity child will tend to jump up often and move around to get a drink or something else.

Some children prefer highly active games or move actively no matter what they do." A high-energy child may have difficulty sitting still in class, whereas a child with low energy can tolerate a very structured environment. The former may use gross motor skills like running and jumping more frequently. A child with a lower activity level may rely more on fine motor skills, such as drawing and putting puzzles together.

Adaptability refers to how long it takes the child to adjust to change over time, as opposed to an initial reaction. Does the child adjust to the changes in their environment easily, or is the child resistant? A child who adjusts easily may be quick to settle into a new routine; a resistant child may take a long time to adjust to the situation.

Approach or *withdrawal* refers to how the child responds to experiences and stimuli, including new people or situations. "Some children tend in new situations to feel immediately comfortable—an approach reaction. Some feel uncomfortable and hold back until they feel comfortable." A bold child tends to approach things quickly, as if without thinking, whereas a cautious child typically prefers to watch for a while before engaging in new experiences.

Persistence and *attention span* refer to the child's length of time on a task and ability to stay with the task through frustrations. A high-persistent child will continue on a task and return to it in spite of distractions and interruptions. A low-persistent child will lose interest more quickly and may leave the task unfinished.

Regularity refers to biological rhythms, including sleep, hunger and bowel movements. "Some children are very regular in biological functions and sleep, wake and eat at the same times each day." Others may go to sleep at different times, have irregular sleep patterns and eat at odd times during the day.

Distractibility refers to how easily a child is drawn away from an activity. Some children will play intently or focus on a learning task and not notice someone walking by; another may be easily sidetracked and find it difficult to focus on the task in hand.

Mood refers to the child's general tendency to be positive or negative in outlook—how often the child is happy, cheerful, joyful, and pleasant or the opposite. "Some children are happy most of the time and a joy to be with. Others are more often unhappy and can be a trial for their parents." Within this particular framework, mood is probably closest to what I refer to as disposition.

All children have all nine traits and many more. How these attributes combine determines a child's unique behavioral style or temperament. Incidentally, the English word *temperament* comes from the Latin *temperare,* which means "to mix." The implication is that temperament is a balance of different elements and not a single characteristic. How would you rate your own mix of attributes?

Adjusting the Attitudes of Others

Sometimes the challenges you face are not in your own attitudes but in those of the people around you. Just because you're expected to achieve benchmarks in a certain way and by a certain time doesn't mean that this is the only path to follow. Sometimes having a positive attitude is about flouting convention. For example, if you want to make your mark as a film actor, most people in the industry would advise you that you'd better be on your way to doing it while you're in your twenties—thirties at the outside.

Anyone considering starting a career in front of the camera in her sixties might have more success trying to fly.

If experts gave this advice to Mimi Weddell, she thankfully didn't listen to them. Until she was sixty-five, Weddell worked in newspapers and advertising, did a little print-ad modeling, raised two children, and appeared in the occasional off-Broadway play. When her husband died in 1981, though, Weddell decided to make acting a priority. She wound up appearing in ten films, including Woody Allen's *The Purple Rose of Cairo* and the Will Smith hit *Hitch,* and doing guest spots on *Sex and the City* and *Law and Order.* She was also the subject of the acclaimed documentary *Hats Off,* a reference to the more than one hundred and fifty hats she owned and regularly sported in public.

"Mrs. Weddell's film roles could perhaps be described as small, some even minute, but only by the literal-minded," the *New York Times* said of her. "For the few moments that the camera lingered on her, she radiated Norma Desmond-like star power."

For the next three decades, at a time when many seriously contemplate retirement, Weddell ratcheted her activity up to a level that would have left those half her age exhausted. She was a regular presence at "cattle call" auditions that are known for being draining all-day events. She maintained strenuous exercise and dance routines. And she did it with such a sense of style and grace that, when she was ninety, *New York* magazine named her one of the fifty most beautiful people in that city.

In the process, she inspired a vast range of people who might have otherwise thought they were too old to do what they wanted to do. Jyll Johnstone, the director of *Hats Off,* noted that she received numerous letters from people who, through her example, Weddell motivated to follow their dreams. "It's amazing how she touched so many lives," Johnstone told the *Los Angeles Times.*

For the entirety of her ninety-four years, and especially the last third of her life, during which she turned her back on what was expected of a woman her age, Mimi Weddell embraced the notion that you face your challenges with an attitude of possibility. "Rise above it is what one does," she says in *Hats Off.* "We're not supposed to be happy, happy, happy and jumping for joy every second." But even when we're not happy, Weddell believed our goal should be to live a life that thrills us. "You dance as you walk through life. If you don't dance, for heaven's sake, you don't lift up from this Earth."

Jef Lynch, Ellen McArthur, Sue Kent and Mimi Weddell all show in their different ways that it's not only aptitude and passion that lie at the heart of finding your Element. It's also your attitude. Your biology and background may define your starting point, but not your destination. Whatever your situation, it's always easier of course to make excuses than to actually do something. As the political activist Antonio Gramsci once said, "The man who does not want to act says that he cannot." But if you are inclined to act, self-belief and determination are a match for the most unpromising beginnings and the most challenging circumstances.

How you respond to the world around you deeply affects how the world responds to you. If you act differently in the world, you may find that new people come into your life, and that the ones you know already reframe you. New opportunities turn up. If you take them, you effect changes in other people's lives as well as your own. This is how the organic nature of human life evolves. Whether and how you become part of that process is a question of attitude.

Some questions to consider:

- How much do you want to be in your Element?
- How hard are you willing to work to get there?

- Do you believe you deserve to find your Element?
- What can you do to raise your belief in yourself?
- How is your temperament affecting your pursuits?
- What can you do to change the attitudes of those around you?

CHAPTER SEVEN

Where Are You Now?

As we saw in the last chapter, some obstacles to finding your Element may be more imagined than real. Of course, everyone's situation is different, and some obstacles may be all too real. In this chapter we look at the external constraints and opportunities that you may be facing. I suggest some ways of taking stock of where you are now, of the resources you have already and of those you may need. It's important to recognize first that we all have different starting points. Whatever yours is may influence the initial direction you take, but it doesn't in itself determine your destination. We'll come to your own situation in a moment. Before we do, let me illustrate the point with some dogleg turns in my own story.

The Leaving of Liverpool

When I was in elementary school in the 1950s, the thought wouldn't have occurred to anyone, least of all me, that I would eventually live in California doing what I do now. As a teenager, I used to go to a folk music club in Liverpool and join in throaty choruses of sea shanties, the general drift of which was that I was done with roving, whiskey and wild, wild women. I'd hardly roved at all at that point and hadn't actually met a wild woman, so far as I knew. That didn't stop me vowing to give them all up. One of the staples of the repertoire was a song called "The Leaving of Liverpool," which began like this.

> *Farewell to Princes landing stage,*
> *River Mersey fare thee well.*
> *I am bound for California,*
> *A place I know right well.*
> *So fare thee well, my own true love,*
> *When I return united we will be.*
> *It's not the leaving of Liverpool that grieves me*
> *But my darling when I think of thee.*

At the time, I didn't know California right well, and I had no idea I was bound for it. Nothing seemed less likely, but here I am. Like all journeys, mine began with the first few steps and evolved through various different phases. Sometimes one grew naturally from another. Sometimes there were conflicting crossroads and a decision to go one way or the other would have led me to a completely different life.

In the summer of 1972, I sat at such a crossroads. Actually, I was sitting in a bar in a public house in Wakefield, England. I was having a pint of beer and contemplating my future. I was twenty-two, unreasonably attractive and had just graduated from college. I had a degree in English, Drama, and Education and a teaching qualification. I had no responsibilities and no attachments. I had been in an intense two-year relationship with a girl in college, but that was over. (Unbelievably, she broke up with me. I know it's hard to imagine, but there it is.) I was under no pressure from my parents to move in any particular direction. As long as I was happy in what I did, they were, too. So what was it to be?

I was musing on two quite different options: to take a teaching job in Sweden or to study for a higher degree in London. I enjoyed teaching and was good at it. I wanted to travel and had applied for a job teaching English to young adults in Sweden. I was attracted by the idea of spending time in Stockholm, by the salary (since I'd never had one), and by the awful plight of so many young Swedish women being unable to speak my mother tongue.

I had also applied for a studentship to study for a PhD at the University of London Institute of Education. I had no long-term aim in studying for a doctorate. The idea just appealed to me. It sounded challenging, like climbing Annapurna. Plus, if you succeeded, you got to call yourself Dr. and I liked the sound of that. The college I went to, Bretton Hall in Yorkshire, had an inspirational principal, Dr. Alyn Davis. He was the first doctor I'd encountered who couldn't write prescriptions. I was impressed. He encouraged me to go down this route and advised me how and where to apply.

As I sat in the pub, I was waiting to hear back from Stockholm and from London. I wasn't sure which option I preferred until the day I had to choose. I received a firm offer from Sweden and they needed a reply within the week. As the week wore on, I still hadn't heard about the studentship. I realized then what I really wanted to do and let the Swedish option go. It was several weeks before I was called for an interview in London and some months before I was offered the studentship I wanted. I moved to

London and set off down the path that has led me, among many other things, to write this book and to my current life in California, which I now know right well.

Getting Out More

When I was twenty-two, I was unencumbered and free to make decisions just for myself. That may be your situation now, in which case you should celebrate it and take full advantage of it. Equally, you may be committed in every direction and feel that your options are much more limited. Even so, dramatic changes of direction are always possible. Many people move countries to change their prospects. I live in the United States now and this land is filled with people from other countries who came here purposefully, often up against terrible hardships, to change their circumstances and to enhance their lives. Not everyone fulfilled their dreams: but they were all prepared to take the chance.

It was our intention with *The Element* to move people. As it turns out, we managed to do that—sometimes even physically. In 2008, Lisa and Peter Labon and their four children were living in San Francisco—a place Lisa calls "our favorite city in the world"—when they saw my first TED talk and picked up a copy of *The Element*. They'd been slowly realizing that they needed to do something very different with their lives, and the book provided further impetus. "It was life-saving nectar from a deeply hidden well," Lisa told me. "Not only did we not want schools to kill our children's creativity, we recognized our own abandoned dreams and withered passions in the dustbin of modern achievement.

"Peter was working long, difficult hours. After fifteen years in money management, he was seriously burning out. I was wrangling four precious children, attempting to manage their development, our household, and family social obligations like a three-ring circus. We were exhausted and isolated in a city full of people juggling the same crazy schedules.

"One of the big moments for me was going to a lecture at the Sacred Heart school. The speaker asked the audience what they wanted for their children. People said things like, 'We want our children to be happy,' 'We want our children to be healthy,' 'We want them to have good relationships.' Then she told us that children say that their parents want them to have a big house, an expensive car, and the right high-paying job. There's a real disconnect between what we're imparting, wishing, and modeling, and the message that's really being sent. We were at a point where we wanted integrity in every part of our life, and we realized that we needed to change everything. We were so enamored with the school our kids were at, but we started to see that it was healthy for children to be challenged in different ways and to stretch outside of the comfortable little bubble we created. It was a liberating moment for us as a family."

What followed was the kind of thing so many people talk about doing, but rarely have the fortitude to do—the Labons dropped everything and reignited their lives. "Our entire family had a simultaneous awakening," Lisa said. "I asked the children if they were happy in their triple-A-rated educational institution and they shrugged. I asked if they would like to travel, and their faces lit up like bonfires. So, full of inspiration, we left our home of fifteen years for the great unknown. We sold our house just as the markets were collapsing, packed up everything, and hit the road."

Lisa loved surfing, so the family went to Sayulita, Mexico, because friends told them the surfing was great. Peter wanted to live in a skiing town, so they rented a house in Aspen for the ski season. Other places followed while Lisa home-schooled the kids. "We had to home-school because we weren't going to be anyplace long enough to get into a school. That was a little scary, but also exciting. My oldest daughter, who was in fourth grade at the time, introduced me to e-schooling. It was a whole new world. I would do it again in a heartbeat, but it was a lot of work.

"Initially we thought we would travel for a few years. There were so many places to visit, things to see and do, experiences to share. The joy of travel quickly waned as the pressure of keeping everyone safe and healthy in new places, not to mention all the packing and unpacking, grew into its own stressor. We traveled for one year, but during that time I asked Peter to think about where 'home' was eventually going to be."

As they journeyed across North America, they continued to consider that question. Lisa identified a handful of qualities required of any future home: a small, healthy community, excellent educational options and an abundance of the nature, sun and outdoor activities the entire family loved. They drew from their experience, they polled friends, they pored over websites like city-data.com, and they did regular gut checks. What they ultimately decided was that their ideal living environment was about eight hundred miles northeast of San Francisco in Park City, Utah.

"One thing that stood out to me was the commitment and devotion of the people who choose to live in mountain towns. They are very clear about what they value in their lives and often make sacrifices to live there. Not simply the colder climate, but also financially. Many artists, intellectuals, and cultural creatives scrape out a living in tourist industries in order to share the mountain trails and fresh air with other locals. The passion for life is palpable in these consciously created communities."

The Labons love their new home, and they've made friends with "extraordinary people." When they were hunkered down in San Francisco, they couldn't have imagined that the place where they were meant to live was in the mountains, away from the ocean and away from the world of finance. By taking a good look at where they were and where they wanted to be (both emotionally and physically), they made the most important move of their lives.

Figuring Out Where You Are

The Labons discovered that you're never as "dug in" as you think you might be. Peter had a responsible position. Lisa had deeply established roots in the Bay Area. The kids had school, friends and lifestyles to which they'd grown accustomed in a city that has a tremendous amount to offer. When they realized that they weren't living the lives they were meant to be living, they could have easily settled for the belief—as so many people do—that their commitments were too great and that their paths were already laid out for them. Instead, they chose to do something exponentially more dramatic, exponentially more challenging and exponentially more fulfilling.

They had every excuse to stay in San Francisco; life was, in many ways, very good for them there. But their Element was somewhere else.

They also learned that starting points can be arbitrary. That they started in San Francisco was nothing more than circumstance. They could have launched their journey from New York, Mali, Liverpool or anywhere else. Similarly, they could have started when the kids were very young, when one of them had gone off to college or when a few of them had yet to be born. What is instructive about their story is not where or when it happened, but that a realization inspired them to head off on their quest. This speaks to all people trying to find their Element: while it's important to look at the obstacles in front of you and while it is essential to take stock of your situation, you can move toward the life you feel you should be living from virtually anywhere. An essential first step here is to take stock of where you are right now.

What's Your Situation?

One commonly used way of taking stock of your current situation is through a SWOT analysis. SWOT stands for strengths, weaknesses, opportunities and threats. The SWOT framework was developed in the sixties by Albert Humphrey, an American business consultant. Although it was originally designed for business, it's widely used by coaches and mentors to help individuals assess their own circumstances and to develop their own plans for personal or professional development. A SWOT analysis helps you assess the internal and external factors that may be helping or hindering you in finding your Element.

Exercise Twelve: Where Are You Now?

To do your own analysis, draw a large square on a piece of paper and divide it into four equal boxes. Name the top left box "strengths," the top right box "weaknesses," the bottom left "opportunities" and the bottom right "threats." Broadly speaking, the two top boxes—strengths and weaknesses—are about your own personal qualities and characteristics; they deal with internal factors. The bottom two are about your practical circumstances;

they deal with external factors. These aren't exclusive categories. You may well see strengths in your circumstances, for example, and threats in your attitudes. But it's useful to keep this general emphasis in mind as you work through this exercise.

Look first at the two upper boxes. Drawing on all the exercises you've done so far, list in these boxes your relative strengths and weaknesses as you see them. Start with your aptitudes. Then in a different color list the strengths and weaknesses in your passions. In a third color, add your strengths and weaknesses in terms of your attitudes. Now look at the bottom two boxes and make a list of the opportunities and of the threats and difficulties you face in your current circumstances. Below are some questions that may prompt you as you complete the boxes.

Consider your basic situation:

- How old are you?
- What are your personal responsibilities?
- What are your financial responsibilities?
- How much of a safety net do you have in terms of family and money?
- How easily can you manage a risk, given everything you have going on in your life?

The next step moves beyond the basics into more nuanced questions:

- How much does it bother you that you feel that you aren't doing the thing that you're meant to be doing?
- If you're reading this book, it may be because you haven't found your Element yet. How much does that truly matter to you, though? Is it something you think would

be nice to have, like a surprise gift basket delivered to your door? Is it a dull ache such as the one Randy Parsons talked about when discussing his life before guitar-making? Or is it something more persistent than that, a voice that reminds you regularly that you're not where you want to be?

Next, consider the biggest obstacles in your way:

- What's keeping you from doing what you really want to do?
- What would it require to get over these hurdles?
- What would the consequences be of jumping over them?

Give these questions some serious thought. Sometimes our obstacles are truly substantial—sick family members depending on your time and financial assistance, the need to stay in a particular location because loved ones wouldn't be able to make the move with you—but often making a significant change has fewer consequences than you might think. Would your partner leave you if you gave up your current job to do something completely different, perhaps for less money? If so, that's a considerable consequence.

Examining the true consequences of overcoming your obstacles is a tremendously important exercise. What would really happen if you decided to follow your dreams? The answer is often less daunting that it first seems.

Now think about your available resources:

- What's available to you right now that could help you pursue your passions?

- If you made an all-out effort to do what you believe you should be doing with your life, what paths are already available to you?

The next step is to consider each of the items in your list in more detail and to ask yourself how you can develop and make the best of your strengths:

- Do you need more time to develop them? More training?
- Do you need different opportunities to discover them or develop them?
- What about your perceived weaknesses? Do other people agree with you about them?
- How do you know they're weaknesses?
- How much do they really matter and, if they do, what can you do to remedy them?

One Door Closes and Another Opens

Taking stock of where you are is essential to getting a new perspective on where you want to be. That was the experience of Mariellen Ward. After a series of losses and traumas in her life, she found a new direction only after an extensive process of soul-searching. "I spent a huge part of my adult life, instead of working at a job and building a savings account, deciding what I was put on this Earth to do," she told me. "I made that my mission in my life. I think it's important to throw yourself into this process fully. Other than my health, I've put everything else aside to go into it. Moneymaking was a sideline for me. I had a degree in journalism and I've worked in the communications field. I always toyed with being a writer. When I look back now, I realize I always wanted to be a writer, but I didn't have the confidence. So I went into jobs that skirted on the edge of what I wanted to do."

Mariellen had two considerable obstacles to overcome. One was that she'd been shuttled through the educational system far too quickly. Because she was academically bright, she skipped two full grades. While she was up to this challenge intellectually, she was not up to it emotionally, as she was surrounded by people who were at different levels of maturity than she was. "My whole education was just botched," she said. "It's taken my whole adult life to recover from my education."

The other huge issue was that, as an adult, she faced a string of traumatic losses that threw her entire life out of whack. "My father went bankrupt and we lost our family cottage. A few months later, my mom died suddenly, and I discovered her body. It was a horrible shock. Not long after that, my fiancé left me. Then my dad died of cancer. I'd be starting to get up off the floor and then I'd be flattened again."

When she was finally able to move forward enough to think about healing, she sought comfort in yoga. "I would go to class and all of my feelings of grief would overcome me and my teacher would allow me to experience it. She offered three classes a week, and I went to each, no matter what. I started breathing, and I started moving. It took a couple of years, but I started coming out of my depression. I knew organically that it was time to go after my dreams."

Finally, after decades of doing things other than what she felt she was meant to be doing, Mariellen started reaching out for opportunities. And when she focused on what she should do, she came away with an overwhelming compulsion to go to India. "It was the strongest inner voice I ever heard in my life. When you hear a voice that strong, you have to follow it. You almost have no choice because your whole being aligns to that. It took a year of planning, saving, putting my things in storage, giving up my apartment."

At the end of that year, Mariellen headed east, unsure of what would be waiting for her. She'd heard plenty of stories about how difficult it was to travel in India, and while the voice inside of her had been emphatic, it hadn't been particularly clear. She knew she had to go to India, but she wasn't sure what was waiting for her there. She'd even begun to wonder if she were going there to die.

"I had this idea that the whole thing would be a long, protracted dark night of the soul. What happened, though, was the exact opposite. I had this absolutely amazing time. I felt that the entire trip I was blessed and protected, and I had one wonderful experience after another. I was throwing myself off a cliff to see if the net would appear. The net not only appeared, but it turned into a magic carpet."

While in India, Mariellen rediscovered her passion for writing. As it turned out, though she was Canadian and of British descent, what she was really meant to do was write about this land.

"All the dots started to connect. I remembered that, from childhood, I was fascinated with the mysterious East. All these dreams of childhood had been obscured, but they hadn't disappeared. For the first time in my life, I just started to write. I realized that this was what I loved to do and what I wanted to do, and I've gotten incredible feedback from people confirming that I'm good at it. When I write about India, I'm connecting to something that's so much bigger than me. It's been worth devoting my entire adult life to discovering this."

Mariellen now writes constantly. "I can't even imagine what writer's block is like." She's created the blog BreatheDreamGo, subtitled "tales of travel and transformation," and the blog is generating both traffic and acclaim, recently receiving nominations for three Canadian Weblog Awards. The next frontier for Mariellen is extending her writing to book form. She's still trying to find a way to make a steady living from her work, but she has no doubts about what she should be doing and no regrets about taking the leap necessary to pursue her opportunities.

To get a better sense of her outward journey, Mariellen had to travel inward first. Her time practicing yoga helped her to assimilate the traumas and grief of the previous years and to emerge from the depression that was shrouding her hopes for the future. Those experiences could have immobilized her. Instead they eventually gave her a greater sense of resilience.

As Joseph Campbell says, if you move in the direction of your passions, opportunities tend to appear that you couldn't have imagined and that weren't otherwise there. Let me add a caveat. Some people do need the special support that can come through personal counseling and therapy. Shortly after *The Element* was published, I was in Seattle to give a public talk and book signing. There were several hundred people in the audience and during the question-and-answer session a young man stood up and asked nervously how he could find his Element. He was clearly agitated and I asked him to tell us a little about his situation. He said that he'd just been discharged from the U.S. military and was angry that there had been no real support or mentoring to help people like him find his true calling back in civilian life. He felt that he and his fellow soldiers had been "pretty much hung out to dry." Recognizing that he really needed to talk, I suggested that we meet for a few minutes at the end of the session. We did and he told me he'd been in Iraq and that he had been trained as an interrogator.

He was twenty-two years old. He'd joined the Army at eighteen when his mother died and he'd been left on his own. He had been devastated to lose his mother and turned to the military for a sense of security. I could only imagine the experiences he had had as an interrogator; what he had seen and been required to do. He was clearly in a very tense, emotional state and said he had been deeply affected by the arguments I put forward in *The Element* and felt that I had offered him a positive way ahead. I hope that proved to be true for him. I also felt that he needed sustained support to deal with experiences that were so traumatic. The exercises and tools in this book can complement such programs, but they are not meant to be a substitute for them. It's for you to understand and decide what you most need in your own unique situation.

Where Do You Want to Go?

It's likely that the quest for your Element won't take you to India. It's entirely possible that it won't even take you out of your house. For my collaborator, Lou Aronica, for instance, his quest involved no longer spending three hours a day commuting to work and instead walking into his home office where he could pursue his career as a writer. Regardless of the distance, though, once you understand where you are and where you want to go, it's essential that you figure out a way to get there.

Some of this comes down to mindset. What do you need to do to prepare yourself for this emotionally? Many people spend a great deal of time imagining themselves following a particular pursuit without ever imagining how that pursuit will make them feel on a day-to-day basis. For example, if your dream has always been to teach, are you prepared for the plethora of mood changes any single day will bring—from the joy of breaking through with one student to the frustration of being unable to get across to another to the frenzy of an overactive classroom? If your new project requires you to operate in a completely different environment, have you prepared yourself for such a dramatic change? Having a hundred colleagues obviously involves a very different dynamic from working by yourself. Similarly, if you're accustomed to spending a great deal of time in your car, are you ready for an endeavor that involves staying in one place for six or seven hours at a time?

Don't underestimate the need for this preparedness. I regularly talk to people who have started to do the thing they believe they should be doing, but are worried that they might have made a mistake because they hadn't prepared themselves emotionally as they should have. Any new situation requires some time for adjustment, but you'll be far better off if you understand beforehand how much of an adjustment you need to make.

Another key step along the way is to identify what kind of experience you need before you can truly pursue your passion. It's often assumed, for example, that to be successful, you have to go to college. Well, you don't. Very many people who have had highly successful and fulfilling lives did not go to college. Others did go and then dropped out before completing the program. I'm not recommending that you shouldn't go to college or that you should drop out if you do. Plenty of people benefit from a college education and for some careers it is essential. On balance, college graduates also tend to earn more money over the course of their lives, but not always.

What I am saying is that you shouldn't assume that going to college will guarantee your future or that not going will undermine it. I know many students who drifted from high school to college without any real understanding of why they were going or what they hoped to get from the experience. They and their parents and teachers simply took it for granted that this was the next required step. Many college students ramble through the experience and graduate with no clearer understanding of what they want to do with the lives than when they enrolled.

The facts, I think, are these. Some paths through life do not depend at all on having a conventional college education. Some people prefer to get into the world of work right away after high school. Second, many people get much more from college if they do something else before they go. I used to teach in a university in England, and I often found that the so-called mature students—those who were taking programs after other work experience—applied themselves with more energy to their studies than younger students who'd gone straight from school. This was because they knew why they were taking the program and were determined to get as much as possible from it. If you're in high school now and you're thinking of going to college but you're not sure what you want to do there, you might consider taking time out of formal education for a year or two to broaden your experiences and give yourself time to breathe.

Ben Strickland is an astrophysics senior at the University of Oklahoma. He agrees:

Those who go directly into college from high school can lose time otherwise spent developing a plan and getting to know themselves better. . . . I am a strong advocate for breaks in education. That's not to say it's best for everyone, but it's certainly not best for everyone to just plow through from kindergarten to a bachelor's degree and beyond. . . .

Many people fear the idea of taking a year off between high school and college—it's practically pounded into our heads that people who do so are not likely to ever attend a university. Those who don't have a "college attending" mention after their names at senior graduation are often viewed as inadequate or lesser. Turning eighteen is supposed to signify the entrance into adulthood, but this isn't the case for everyone. . . .

I wasn't ready after high school. Every sign pointed to yes. I had great grades, great AP test scores, great SAT/ACT scores and I was eighteen years old—seems like a short list to judge a college entrant by, doesn't it? I came, I tried to look busy while having close to no clue what I was doing and I managed to hang around for three years. It was entirely too long if you ask me. . . .

After taking around three years off and working with my hands in a very satisfying blue-collar job, I'm back. This time, I have a purpose and understand the concepts of hard work and responsibility to my fellow humans. There are many like me who, in their first attempt, floundered, but went out into the world, grew and returned to kick some real ass. . . .

One of the most genuine and compassionate people I'm lucky enough to know took a one-year break because he had the awareness and maturity to realize he wasn't really working towards a purpose. "I was just walking down a path with no real drive or reason," he told me. "It took my leaving college to recognize my desire to be a therapist. Knowing that goal, I have seen the path I need to follow to get there." Now in the school of social work, he says he's "realized his love for helping people." . . .

Another friend took a year off between high school and college to take a tour of the south in a van with bunch of "skateboarding hooligans." After returning and working in a metal shop for several months and building a financial foundation, he purports, "Then I remembered: Oh yeah! I should go to college." Now you can find him lurking around the physics and math quadrant, hair ablaze as he teases apart mathematical proofs and the inner workings of the universe. . .

The truth is this: there is much to be gained by spending time other ways than rigorously studying. College is hardly the only source of education in life. And while you're truly lucky to have this opportunity, if you take a break and see the world, college will still be here when you get back—and who knows, you might just find a purpose.

My third point is that there are many more options in higher education than conventional academic programs. So-called vocational colleges—in design, performing arts, trades and industries, for example—have a huge amount to offer students of all ages. The culture of academicism has tended to demean work of this sort, even though our economies depend on them and many people find their true calling in them.

Sometimes the requirements of being in your element are very subtle. When Lou embarked on his writing career, he assumed he had all the prerequisites. After all, as a publisher, he'd been working with writers for two decades and he'd been writing constantly. However, his first couple of efforts at prose fell flat. It took him a bit of time to realize that this was because everything he wrote read like an interoffice memo. He'd become so steeped in that form of communication that it had infiltrated everything he put on the page. He needed to retrain himself to write like a writer rather than a corporate employee.

Another thing to consider is how you're going to make this move. Are you going to dive in, or are you going to put a toe in the water? Can you start your journey while maintaining your old job, as Yasmin Helal did when she started Educate-Me, or does it require making a complete break, as the Labons did when they headed off on their travels? Much of this will depend on a variety of factors you'll probably have considered by the time you get to this point: your sense of comfort with change, your financial safety net, the support of friends and family, and how desperate you are to be fully engaged on your journey.

Finally, it's important for you to have a plan for dealing with the predictable challenges (as opposed to the challenges you can't predict, which everyone faces). How are you going to address detractors? How are you going to navigate through financial difficulties? What will you do the first time your lack of experience throws up a wall in front of you?

As you can see, there are many moving parts here. They all confirm a point that's made in every story in this book: there is no single route to finding your Element. Life is not linear. It is organic.

Here are some final questions to consider as you look around and take stock of where you are now and where you might like to move next:

- How easily can you take a risk?
- What are the biggest hurdles?
- What would it take to get over them?

- What would happen if you did?
- What would happen if you didn't?
- Will your loved ones support you or oppose you?
- How do you know?
- Are you ready?

CHAPTER EIGHT

Where's Your Tribe?

THERE'S NO ONE in the world precisely like you, nor is there anyone else living your life. However, there may be many people who share your interests and passions. Part of being in your Element is finding out what world you want to be in— what sort of culture you enjoy and who your "tribes" are. In this chapter we look at the power of tribes in finding your Element and suggest how you can find and connect with yours.

What is a tribe? For our purposes, a tribe is a group of people who share the same interests and passions. The tribe may be large or small. It can exist virtually, through social media or in person. Tribes may be highly diverse. They may cross generations and cultures. They may cross time and include people who are no longer living but whose lives and legacy continue to inspire those who are. You may be a member of various tribes at the same time or at different points in your life. What defines tribes are their shared passions.

Connecting with people who share your Element can have tremendous benefits for you and for them. They include *affirmation, guidance, collaboration* and *inspiration*. We'll look at each of these as we go on, with a range of examples from very different sorts of activity. Let's begin with an example of a tribe that interestingly illustrates an apparent paradox.

Dale Dougherty understood the power of tribes when he decided to launch a magazine aimed at people with a reputation for being solitary—people who tend to spend far more time sequestered in basements and garages than connecting with their fellow travelers. The magazine, *Make*, is aimed at inventors and tinkerers.

"When we started the magazine," Dale told me, "the idea was to look at how people were taking Google and using it for their own purposes. I was fascinated with things like TiVo hacks, where people were taking apart their TiVos and upgrading them. I started looking for things like these and I realized we have a generation of people who have grown up with technology and love playing with it and figuring out what it's about. I thought I could do a magazine about what you could do with technology. In many ways, it's a reinvention of what *Popular Mechanics* and *Popular Science* did in the fifties. I feel that we lost that in our culture for a while."

Make found its tribe immediately. As I'm writing this, the quarterly has published more than thirty editions, has a strong online presence and is a leading voice of the "maker movement," a technology-driven, do-it-yourself subculture.

"The idea behind *Make* is that people want to get control of technology and they want it to do something for them specifically. Sometimes that leads to original inventions, and sometimes to something purely functional. The thing that ties it all together is participation. It's one of the ways of telling people who you are. When you do something, you can share it, and people find you and you can find them."

This idea of people finding each other through their inventions led to the creation of the Maker Faire. Billed as "The world's largest DIY festival," Maker Faires gather inventors and innovators from all over the world to show off their creations, be entertained by the creations of others and bathe in an atmosphere of creativity without bounds. There are flagship Maker Faires in Northern California, New York and Detroit, and mini-faires in cities all over North America. In January 2012, the first Australian Maker Faire was held. With the expansion of the locations comes an explosion in the size of the audience: the 2011 faire in California drew seventy thousand people.

The sense of community among the maker movement extends far beyond *Make* and Maker Faires, though. The web is filled with videos of people showing off their inventions, or the way they've upgraded or repurposed existing items. "Kids see what they're doing here as a form of personal expression." Dougherty said. "They can put up a video about how they built something or how it works. I don't see people doing this because they want to save money. They're doing it because they want meaning. It's not just the end result; it's about the process. You're creating value in doing something the way you want it."

The fascinating thing is that as large and supportive as this community is, those within it tend to see themselves on the periphery of society. Dougherty notes, "I was at an entrepreneur conference recently and heard people say that they consider themselves to be outsiders and that they believe that a lot of their power comes from being outside and not wishing too much to be inside. To me, the energy and interest that comes from makers is all on the edges, not in the center. I think it's more interesting to keep pushing the edges out and seeing what's out there."

The Culture of Tribes

Being in your Element is not only about what you do for a living. Some people can't make a living from what they love to do and some don't want to. Like many of those involved in the maker movement, they prefer to pursue their Element as a purely recreational process. If you are considering earning your living from your Element, it's important to bear in mind that you not only have to love what you do; you should also enjoy the culture and the tribes that go with it.

When I was a student in my twenties, I loved to direct plays and I was reasonably good at it, too. Some of my friends assumed I'd try to make my way in the professional theater. I didn't assume that. I enjoyed directing, but I never felt that life in the theater was for me. I love and admire performers and directors, but there is something in the rhythm and dynamics of the life they lead that doesn't resonate with me.

I mentioned earlier that my father assumed when I was little that I would be the natural soccer player in the family and might even play for our local team, Everton. I didn't, but my youngest brother Neil actually did. He and my brother John were both taken on as apprentices in their teens. Both proved to be highly talented soccer players. Neil went on to a full professional career. John, who had all the same talents as a player, didn't enjoy the culture of the professional game. He's still an ardent fan and continued to play and coach in other capacities for many years. But he didn't connect to the particular rhythms and rituals of the life of an apprentice. Instead, he became more focused on working with people and has had a lifelong interest in food and nutrition. Both he and Neil have been committed vegans since their early teens—not least because of one of my early attempts at haute cuisine involving a largely inedible rabbit pie. Incidentally, for Neil, being vegan also proved a point of tension with the dominant culture of professional soccer. Tribes aren't always a perfect fit. But they do need to be good enough to sustain your connection.

Who do you imagine your tribe to be? What sorts of communities attract you and what is it that you have in common with them? To explore these questions, try this exercise.

Exercise Thirteen: Imagine Your Tribe

Make a vision board of the people and communities that attract your interest:

- Who do you associate with your Element?
- What is it about them that you find interesting?
- Do you think of particular personality types?
- Or is your focus more on what they actually do?
- What matters for you in a tribe?
- Is it playfulness, humor, intensity, irreverence?
- Is it all of these and more or a different set of characteristics altogether?

Affirmation: Growing Together

We are organic creatures and many of the dynamics of other forms of organic life apply to us, too. For example, different types of plants sometimes grow better when they are near each other. In gardening, this phenomenon is known as companion planting. In an article in *Flower and Garden* magazine, Jeffrey S. Minnich explains that "Plants, like people, get along with one another in many ways. Sometimes two different plants get along well as neighbors. Sometimes plants growing near each other don't get along. At other times plants actually help each other to grow."

Similarly, members of tribes, however various and diverse they may be, can help each other to flourish. Finding your tribe is a powerful validation of your own interests and passions. It affirms and reinforces your commitment to what you're doing and can relieve the sense of isolation that people sometimes feel without such a connection. If you're with the wrong tribe you may find yourself starting to wilt, and that the juice is being sucked out of you, too. That's what happened to Neroli Makim. She had to move away from one set of tribes to find a different culture that allowed her talents to flourish.

You don't always find your Element just where you are. Sometimes, you need to travel further down the road. For Neroli, that road started in a cattle station in Australia. "I grew up in a really isolated place," she told me, "and what that meant was that we didn't have stuff that normal people had. We didn't have television, we didn't have electricity for a while, we had diesel-generated motors that we turned off at night. We had very bad roads where you could be cut off for three months of the year. This meant we had to be very creative. You had no external input. We just had to use our imaginations. I found I would draw a lot to relieve boredom. I used to write stories to go with the pictures."

Eventually, Neroli moved closer to the rest of civilization. She went to boarding school, and then to university. Interestingly, no matter how far she traveled and how many people she met, she found that drawing, writing, and the other expressions of creativity she'd developed while she had little contact with the outside world were still what interested her the most. As it turns out, she'd found her passion very early, but didn't realize that until she tried a number of other things on for size.

"School was great fun for the first few years. I'd been home-schooled until I was twelve. I went to boarding school, and for the first time I was going to have a lot of kids my age to be around. It was a grand adventure. But I soon decided that school was an 'oppressive regime.' After graduation, I tried every now and then to go to a nine-to-five job, and I literally thought it would kill me. I would rather have jumped off a bridge than do that. I've never been able to handle being in a very controlled environment. I need to do what I love doing without being controlled."

She eventually realized that creativity itself was her passion, and that sharing it with others was her life's work. She launched a company called Your Creative Success and published a book ti-tled *Your Inner Knowing: Unlocking the Secrets to Creative Success*; her paintings and sculptures have been exhibited internationally; and she speaks regularly on the topic of creativity.

She doesn't love every aspect of her job—there are few in the world that do—but she loves far more than she doesn't. "The stuff that feels right really outweighs the stuff that feels wrong. Whatever I'm doing, I think it really matters. It's so important and interesting to me. When I had other jobs, I knew they were wrong because the things I was doing didn't matter to me. I wasn't inspired by them, and I didn't believe in them."

Trying Tribes on for Size

As I said earlier, one of the things you need to accept before you can truly feel that you are in your Element is that you enjoy the lifestyle that goes with it. "Trying a tribe on for size" is a way of discovering if you can truly be in this world over the long haul. When you start spending time with other people who are doing what you think might be your passion, do you feel more excited or less? Are you discovering baggage that comes with the pursuit that you hadn't considered—and that you're not entirely comfortable with? Conversely, are you seeing opportunities that you'd never pondered before and that make you even more excited about being a part of this world? Discovering your tribe and becoming a part of it can shine a bright and revealing light on your element.

Craig Dwyer needed to go a long way to find his tribe: from Toronto to Japan, and from the world of finance to the world of education. "I was working in a bank doing financial services—mortgages, mutual funds, lines of credit, that kind of thing," he told me. "It wasn't like I disliked the job or that I disliked my employer. They were very good to me, they paid me well, and I had a good life, but there was something missing. I wasn't able to be creative and do the things that I like to do. I found that I was really bored. I'm the type of person who needs to be engaged in what he does, and I wasn't engaged. I was just filling out forms and I didn't deal with people all that much. I'd have meetings with people two or three times a week and then spend the rest of my time doing paperwork. It was just putting stuff into the computer and sending it off and waiting for an automated message."

While watching a Japanese movie one night, a light went on for Craig. The idea of living in Japan intrigued him, and he started looking into career possibilities there. When he saw an ad seeking English-language teaching assistants, he applied for it, even though he had no training as a teacher. He didn't know anyone in Japan, and he barely knew the field he was entering, but it felt right to him.

"I was working in an elementary school as an assistant language teacher. Sometimes they let me do things that I could create, and the rest of the time I just did what they told me to do. One teacher assigned me a project, and I created a big market in the gym that was like a Japanese festival. The kids had a great time, and he told me that we had to do more of that. He was the one who encouraged me to do new things and not to simply follow the textbook. That's what really got me interested."

While in Japan, Craig got married and started a family. By this point, he loved teaching so much that he decided that he wanted to get the degree necessary to have his own classroom. He returned to Canada to attend the University of Toronto, and then went back to Japan, realizing that his passion was not only for teaching but also specifically for teaching there.

"Making the original trip to Japan was a huge lifestyle change. I left a job that was incredibly secure and promised a lot of financial rewards if I stuck with it. But I didn't love it. And I think that the passion I have for what I do now is ultimately going to result in the same lifestyle I had before. I'm not just teaching, I'm doing lots of things. I'm working with people on developing lesson plans and textbooks. There are so many options once you get into a field, and there are so many different ways to go. There's so much more to education than just teaching."

In Craig's case, he needed to travel a huge physical distance to confirm his passion. In a very real way, though, it had been waiting for him to notice. As with Neroli, he'd been dabbling in his passion since he was a child. "When I was younger I was a snowboarder. We used to live right near the snowboarding hill in Toronto. I would teach there, because they'd give me a free season pass. Every weekend I would go in and teach little kids and I loved it. I guess I never put things together and thought I should try teaching as a career. In hindsight, those were some of my better days, and when I think back on it now, I realize I'm using a lot of the skills I used back then."

Guidance: Understanding Your Path

Tribes can be a powerful a source of mentoring. When our son James was thirteen he developed a deep interest in Buddhism. He read everything he could find. He studied the principles and precepts of the eightfold path and meditated several times a day. He collected Buddhist figures and set up a small shrine in his bedroom, which became the focus of his daily practice. All of this evolved while he was also obsessed with basketball, music and other regular teenage things.

After several months of immersion in Buddhism, he asked us if there was a Buddhist temple nearby that he could visit. At the time we lived in a detached house deep in the countryside of England about four miles from Stratford-on-Avon, the birthplace of William Shakespeare. The area has many attractions and people come from all over the world to experience them. Buddhism is not high among them. People tend to go to Thailand for that. I didn't think it was likely that we would find a handy Buddhist temple. But we did.

About two miles from our house in a straight line across the field, but four miles by winding country roads, there was an old, beautifully restored farmhouse in a narrow leafy lane. We'd often passed the wooden gates and wondered what lay behind them. It turned out to be a Buddhist temple known as the Forest Hermitage, a national center for Theravada Buddhism.

James and I went to visit it and met the abbot, Ajahn Khe-madhammo, a wonderful, insightful Englishman who'd been a leading figure in his field for more than thirty years. The temple held meditation meetings every week that were open to the public, and he invited James to join them. So began a regular series of twice-weekly visits that continued until we left England for California.

One afternoon, my wife, Thérèse, and I sat at the back of the temple as James took his first precepts in Pali. He went on to become a devoted member of the community. But for his interest, we would never have known of the Temple's existence. But for the abbot's welcome, James would not have developed his interests to such a deep level. His connection with the monks illustrated for all of us the great power of tribes in validating and inspiring personal commitments and their roles in providing mentorship and support. Discovering the temple was also a vivid illustration of the resources that may manifest in the least likely places, when you turn your attention to finding them.

Collaboration: Giving Support

Wherever common interests align, tribes can emerge. Sometimes these tribes serve as a foundation and a support system, such as Matthew Lee's tribe of fellow magicians in the Philippines. At other times, as with makers, the tribe serves as a touch point, a way to share a common interest without any member of the tribe exerting too much influence on any other member. Tribes that work together can achieve more than individuals acting alone because they stimulate each other's creativity and sense of possibility. In *The Element* we called this "the alchemy of synergy."

Being in your Element can take dedication, determination

and a keen sense of self-awareness. It can be tough to sustain the energy and inspiration to keep moving forward. One of the things that a tribe offers is support and peer review. This is what Kimberley Spire-Oh discovered when she set out on a highly specialized legal career.

A diagnosis of ADHD can have a dramatic effect on your career direction. Sometimes, as Kimberley discovered, it can even have a dramatic effect on your mother's career direction. This is what happened when her son's school system told her he had a "disability."

Up to that point, Kimberley had spent a rather uninspired tenure in law. "I went to law school back in '91," she told me, "but I didn't find exactly what I wanted to do. I started out working in a law firm, and I didn't feel that was a good fit for me. Although my law school trained me to represent corporations and big business, I was always looking at social work. Sometimes when I'd interview or apply for jobs I was considered overqualified. Some of the jobs I ended up getting didn't exist, but after they met me and got to know me they figured that my skills could create something that they actually needed in their organization. They hadn't already anticipated to create that position before. That has always worked better for me, because I have so many different interests and because I haven't followed a straight career path. Maybe what I'm looking for isn't very commonly available. Up until now, I have been a work in progress."

This all changed when her son's school began to dictate his fate. They'd originally identified him as a gifted student who just had some issues fitting into the mainstream. Kimberley knew her son was very bright and she could sympathize with this assessment. Then the school's position took a sudden turn. They now believed that he not only had ADHD but also sensory processing issues and speech problems. This was going to completely change the kind of schooling he received and the environment he learned in, and this was absolutely unacceptable to Kimberley. Suddenly her training as a lawyer came into play.

"I had to advocate for him against the school system. I started out by believing that the schools knew how to handle every situation and then realized that they didn't know my son at all and that I had to speak out on his behalf and help them to provide what they needed to do to help him be what he's going to be. I started learning about the law in special education. I looked for assistance when I went up against the school system and felt they weren't doing the right thing in the part of South Florida where I live."

She was able to make a difference in her son's situation, getting him the kind of education he needed. At the same time, she found the driving professional passion she'd previously been missing.

"The more effective I became at advocating for my son, the more people started speaking to me—his doctors, other parents—saying, 'You're a lawyer, you really should do this.' I decided this was a very good match for me."

Kimberley founded her own law firm. Before the run-in with her son's school, Kimberley had given up practicing law completely, taking a job with a legal publisher. She'd considered starting a firm of her own but she didn't think she could pull it off because she lacked court experience. When she started advocating for her son, the light went on, and a conversation with the woman who became her law partner convinced her that she had all the necessary skills. While she also handles consumer law and civil litigation, her practice focuses on special education law and advocacy, as well as disability law.

"Although there are a few people out here in this area who are doing it, a lot of them are, like me, parents of kids with disabilities, and they're just angry about what happened and they go about it in a different way than a mediator would. I guess I'm meeting a need that was unmet. I'm not just going to be handling cases. I'm dealing with nonprofits to train other parents. I'm trying to educate other parents so they don't just sit back and think the school knows best. They have the ability to advocate for their own children and make the schools fit what their child's needs are. This issue is extremely important to me and I think all the different things I've done in the past makes me very effective at it. I enter every situation trying to work with people and I will push it as far as it has to go to get what is needed, but approaching it from a mediator problem-solving viewpoint helped me to stand out and made me very effective."

What was critical to her success and growth, though, was the connection she made to a very specialized tribe: lawyers already doing what she was setting out to do. This tribe offered her much more outside assistance than she ever anticipated.

"I was surprised at how many people are willing to help you and answer questions even though I thought they'd see me as a competitor. This seems to be especially true in a field where you're trying to help people; they want more people out there helping people. They will do everything they can to help you succeed. The other special ed attorneys have been phenomenal."

This is something I hear regularly from people who find their tribes, especially if it's in a specialized or niche undertaking. There's something encouraging about how people who share the same passion will help each other, even if they're potentially vying for the same customers. This is one of the most valuable traits of a tribe: the love for the pursuit tends to outweigh the instinct to protect one's turf. In Kimberley's case, there have been more than enough clients to go around, and the support the tribe offers improves everyone's lot.

Chris Bird learned the collaborative power of tribes when she discovered that she suddenly needed to go back to work. She'd spent eighteen years in advertising and had recently given birth to her daughter. The plan was for her to be a stay-at-home mom in the Denver suburb where she lived, but when her husband became seriously ill, that plan required some adjustment. Being around to take care of her family was nonnegotiable. She went to a career coach for inspiration. She liked writing, technology and design—all skills she'd used in her advertising career—and hoped she could generate an income from these talents. The coach suggested that Chris consider social media, specifically blogging. Chris hadn't thought of this before but the suggestion made sense. She started a mom blog, quickly realizing that to be successful she was going to have to build her community.

"I looked for a network of mom bloggers like myself," she told me, "and found Mile High Mamas, a network that the *Denver Post* has put together online. They were doing local events where bloggers could get together and promote local businesses. I was meeting other moms like me who wanted to be home with their kids but also wanted to use their talents to do something."

Chris was beginning to connect with her tribe. One member of that tribe was Barb Likos, who runs a series of sites under the Chaotic Communications banner and had been blogging practically from the time the form existed. "She was doing it when it was still in HTML," Chris said, which was essentially the social media equivalent of using a stone tablet and a chisel. Chris was thinking about home-schooling her daughter and Barb had been a teacher and was home-schooling her child. The two had a long phone conversation. Eventually the conversation segued into one about blogging, Barb began to convey some of her ideas, and Chris quickly realized that she'd found a much-needed mentor.

"Barb was involved in a group called Mom It Forward, which gets moms to promote businesses and support each other. She was so involved with the social media side, and she told me that I could call her any time. She said it was her policy to share all of her knowledge because it only benefits her in the end to share with others because they would help her by sharing what they know."

Out of a small tribe built from Mile High Mamas a mentorship was born that, with Barb's guidance, has seen Chris grow her business beyond blogging into various forms of social media. Chris now runs a company called BirdBanter Media that helps various clients with their social media needs. She has also evolved her blogging, discovering that she could combine her love for parenting with her love for travel. Her husband, a pilot, is now back in good health, which helps. One of the sites on which her posts appear regularly is TravelingMom.com.

Meanwhile Chris stays strongly connected to her tribe. "Barb decided she would start a group on Facebook of mom bloggers she knew and trusted so she could share her knowledge and we could share back. It has been such a phenomenal group. We share everything. We share what we're writing about. We talk about media trades; about how to pitch PR companies; about software; about tech support and emotional support. It's a place where we can connect immediately in real time. We promote each other's work—we call it 'post pimping.' We talk about what each other charges for services. We share leads for PR and jobs. We share our contact information. We make playdates. We organize mom's nights out. We can disagree and still respect each other because it's a safe place." Chris continues to learn valuable things from her mentor, and her tribe of "mompreneurs" continues to grow and to help each other grow.

Inspiration: Raising the Bar

Finding your tribe can be a tremendous source of inspiration. Seeing what others achieve who share your passion can drive you to push the boundaries of your own work and to raise the bar of your own aspirations. Tribes can help to raise everyone's game. One example is the New Nordic Cuisine movement that started in Scandinavia and is now steadily spreading throughout the world.

There have been great restaurants in Scandinavia for a very long time. The region has a strong and distinctive culinary tradition but it rarely had a significant effect on world food culture. All of that began to change when famed chef and restaurateur Claus Meyer rallied a collection of Scandinavian chefs behind a "Manifesto for the New Nordic Kitchen."

"As Nordic chefs," the manifesto begins, "we find that the time has now come for us to create a New Nordic Kitchen, which in virtue of its good taste and special character compares favorably with the standards of the greatest kitchens of the world." The manifesto set specific goals for high-achieving Scandinavian chefs, ranging from setting elevated standards for freshness and seasonality to promoting animal welfare and developing "potentially new applications of traditional Nordic food products."

The manifesto served as a gathering point for chefs all over the region, most notably Danish chef René Redzepi. Together, Meyer and Redzepi opened Noma, the Copenhagen restaurant that was named San Pellegrino World's Best Restaurant in both 2010 and

2011. Noma is simply the highest-profile venue for the movement. All over Scandinavia, this tribe is pushing the food, and each other, in ever expanding directions. Though in many ways they are competing for the same customer, they also seem to sense that they can build something bigger by supporting each other. And in fact that seems to be the case. Copenhagen in particular has become one of the hottest destinations in the world for culinary tourism.

At a recent MAD Foodcamp, culinary stars—many of whom compete in the same city for the same high-end restaurant-goer—participated in a symposium on New Nordic Cuisine, embracing techniques and philosophies and bringing them back to their homes. Meanwhile, the tribe continues to grow as chefs from all over the world participate in the movement.

The benefits of finding your tribe apply in every field and domain of activity. The world of Nordic cuisine may seem very distant from the world of writing suspense thrillers. It is. But the power of connection is just as strong. Today Ethan Cross is an internationally bestselling suspense writer, author of the thrillers *The Shepherd, The Prophet* and *The Cage.* Just a few years ago, he was walking into the International Thriller Writers' ThrillerFest in Manhattan, not certain that he could make a career out of writing. What he discovered nearly instantly, though, was that he had a home within this tribe.

"It was really incredible to sit there in classes and learn from guys who had sold hundreds of thousands and even millions of copies," he told me. "One thing I found when I first started writing a book is that there are a lot of unwritten rules that you don't learn in English class—things to avoid and things that help bring the reader in better. At ThrillerFest, I learned a lot of things that I was able to apply, and this gave me more confidence right away."

One of the sessions Ethan attended was run by two respected authors about pitching agents. This was invaluable, because Ethan was meeting with agents the next day. His new tribe provided assistance. "That night there was a cocktail party and all the aspiring authors were going around practicing their pitches with each other." The practice pitches went very well for Ethan, giving him an even stronger sense of validation, a greater belief that he had genuine talent.

The next day came PitchFest. "It's essentially like speed-dating with different agents. You go in a big room with agents sitting at tables and you get in line. You get three minutes, after which you have to get up, even if you're in the middle of your pitch, and switch. If agents like the pitch, they'll invite you to send them something." Several agents expressed interest in Ethan's work.

The strongest sense of validation came after the event. Several of the established writers that Ethan met at that first ThrillerFest invited him to send them a chapter of his novel for critique. The comments he received were hugely valuable, but even more valuable was how seriously these writers took him—treating him like a "real" novelist.

Audiences in America and Europe have since confirmed that appraisal. *The Shepherd* was a bestseller in both the United States and UK and has been sold for translation in a half-dozen countries. But the first sense that Ethan had that he was doing what he should be doing came from the tribe he discovered at a New York writers conference.

Finding Your Tribe

So, if you haven't found your tribe yet, how do you go about doing so? Here are some practical possibilities.

USE THE INTERNET

The Internet has evolved into the most comprehensive and dynamic system of communication in the history of humanity. It provides unprecedented opportunities to connect with people who share your interests. Of course, you should keep in mind all the usual warnings about the risks of forming relationships on the Internet and act with proper caution. That said, using it in a creative and focused way can generate enormous amounts of leads and information to help you connect with others who share your element.

There are some drawbacks in spending too much time on social media sites. It might not be a complete coincidence that "Twitter" rhymes with "fritter." But they are extraordinary tools for finding kindred spirits. Type in the phrase "public speaking" in Facebook, for example, and you'll find that tens of thousands of Facebook members have listed that as an interest. Click through, and you might very well find that several of your friends or associates are among this group. "Like" the page, and you immediately become part of this community. Similarly, typing #publicspeaking into Twitter nets a large number of tweets and an equally large number of people you can follow and who are likely to follow you back. Does this mean that you're now part of this tribe? Not really, at least not yet, but it does mean that you are beginning to connect with a community that shares your passion.

A search engine can also help introduce you to your tribe. Type "public speaking" into Google, and you'll get, as of this writing, more than twenty-five million results. Clearly you can't review all of these—everyone knows that anything past the first half million Google results is redundant, anyway—but browsing through the first several pages could lead to some interesting discoveries: organizations, conferences, courses and mentors. Look for particular blogs, clubs, societies and online communities that are close to your interests.

Of course, you may find that your tribe is scattered across several continents. For previous generations this was a problem. It is not now and you should take advantage of the fact. You can gain great validation and inspiration through online communities and membership of virtual tribes. If you type "public speaking" and your hometown, you'll get even closer to a tribe that you might be able to connect with immediately.

This last bit of search might be precisely the thing to take you out of the virtual world of tribes and into the physical one.

TURN UP

Look for clubs and associations that you can visit and attend in person. However valuable online communities can be, there is a different level of energy and connection that comes from being in the same physical space with other people who share your interests. Look in particular for special events and conventions that may feature guest speakers, workshop leaders, displays and exhibitions that provide a focus for contact and conversation. Maybe there's a meet-up group nearby. Perhaps a local symposium is coming up in a few weeks. Tapping into this could allow you to find people who speak your language, love what you love and share your goals.

One of the things we heard from several of the people we interviewed for this book was that they were completely unaware that there were organizations out there built around their interests. Having access to these organizations could change everything for you.

SIGN UP

Consider signing up for short courses or workshops. In most countries, education institutions of all sorts offer short programs, weekend and evening classes, and other public lectures, programs and events. Find out who offers what in your area and sign up for whatever interests you. And remember, going along and trying something out doesn't lock you in. It's voluntary to go and voluntary not to go again if it's not for you. The point is to look with an open heart as well as a critical mind.

VOLUNTEER

In chapter five, I said that genuine happiness often comes from helping others. Wherever there are human communities there are people who need support, and usually organizations of all sorts to help to provide it. There are organizations that focus on every type of social and personal need. In an overwhelming number of cases they depend on volunteers to do the work. There is a double benefit here. The people who need help benefit from you providing it. You benefit too by broadening your range of activities and networks. The principle is always the same: you create new opportunities by taking the ones in front of you.

BE AN INTERN

Be in the world you want to be in. One way is to become an intern for a time. Many organizations now take on interns. If you're skeptical about the reasons some of them have for doing this, you're right to be. There's been a huge increase in the numbers of

internships in the past few years and in some cases they're a cynical source of free labor. Often an intern's work is tedious and
routine. You should check carefully the details of any position
that might interest you and be clear about the terms. With that in
mind, short-term internships can be a great way of getting experience of different work environments and of the cultures that go
with different occupations. If it suits your age and circumstances,
you should look at them seriously.

FIND A MENTOR

If you can afford it, spend some time with an accredited life coach.
In the last twenty years a whole profession has sprung up offering
practical support and techniques to help you clarify and achieve
your purposes in life. As in every profession from medicine to law,
there are great practitioners and not-so-great ones. There are many
different systems, too. Take time to check out prospective coaches
properly. Look at their websites and books if they have any. Check
testimonials and client feedback. If you find the right match for
you, the results can be well worth the investment of your time
and money.

FINDING YOURSELF

Whether it's changing countries or occupations, connecting exclusively online, showing up in person to a group meeting, taking
courses, going to events or volunteering, the value in widening
your sphere of activities is not only in the immediate experience.
It is in the doors that it may open to new experiences and people.
Finding your Element and others who share it can also give you a
new sense of who you really are.

Keith Robinson (no relation) is an animator and illustrator. He'd always done well in school academically and socially, but all of this changed in his third year of secondary school when he started being bullied. "First I was ostracized by my classmates," he told me, "and this was quickly seized upon by the school bullies. For the next couple of years, I did my best to disappear completely. My strategy was to laugh off the playground taunts if I could and to otherwise render myself invisible. This enforced period of introspection made me take a hard look at myself and at the reasons for my change in fortune. I came to realize that my former self-confidence had turned me into a rather obnoxious, loudmouthed show-off. I decided the best strategy for rehabilitation was to remain quiet and unassuming, which ironically did my grades no end of good."

While Keith was learning to cope with his circumstances, he became increasingly interested in art—and in the process discovered a new tribe. "Art classes at school were a refuge. In art class I was with a different group of pupils, neither my regular classmates nor the bullies. I could be a different person (or perhaps, just be myself) and over time I found a different group of friends there, who approached me without prejudice and perhaps with a little admiration because I could draw. I became aware that being able to draw held a special kind of kudos at school, a bit like being good at sport (which I was hopeless at)."

Through this tribe, Keith found a new way to define himself, a way that was perhaps more natural than any other. Eventually, the bullying stopped and his circle of friends widened, thanks in large part to the community he found through art. "Through art, I found a way to reinvent myself. Art had become what I wanted to do and who I wanted to be. It gave me what all adolescents are looking for: an identity."

For Keith, this led to a connection with an even larger tribe. "I made art college my goal, thanks largely to the encouragement of my art teacher, who recognized that I had some ability and a lot of enthusiasm and who showed me that I could actually turn this into a career. He arranged a week's work experience with a local graphic design firm, owned by a tutor at the local art college. It was a revelation to me. The studio was in a beautiful converted barn, nobody wore a suit, and best of all, people spent their days with marker pens and layout pads being creative.

"From that moment I didn't want to do anything else. I loved art college. I was absolutely in my Element. It was a kind of creative boot camp. It tore down everything I thought I knew and liked and taught me how to see and think in a completely new way. I couldn't get enough of it. I still can't."

As with finding your Element, if you're looking for your tribe, you can't plan the whole process. That's the point. Finding your tribe is not a linear process whose outcomes you can predict. It's an organic one that you can only cultivate and propagate. If you do it well, you may find it produces a harvest of new opportunities that you couldn't have anticipated.

Here are some questions to consider:

- What sorts of people do you associate with your Element?
- Do they interest and attract you or not? Do you know why?
- If you know what your Element is, do you want to earn your living from it?
- If you do, what do you feel about the professional culture that goes with it?

- What practical courses or programs of study would interest you?
- What key words would you use for an Internet search to find your tribe?
- How do you feel about joining online groups or communities?
- How do you feel about being a member of groups that meet in person?
- What sorts of groups or events are you interested in attending?
- What qualities would you look for in a coach or mentor?

CHAPTER NINE

What's Next?

I F YOU'VE BEEN engaged actively with this book, by now you'll have given some real thought to your aptitudes and passions, to your attitudes and your current situation. Where do you go from here?

In planning your way forward, it's important to remember the three core principles that are at the heart of my argument. First, your life is unique. You can learn from the experiences of other people, but you cannot and should not try to duplicate them. Second, you create your own life and you can re-create it. In doing that, your greatest resources are your own imagination and sense of possibility. Third, your life is organic, not linear. You can't plan the whole of your life's journey and you don't need to. What you do need to plan are the next steps.

There's an old joke about someone driving through the countryside looking for a village. He stops and asks a local man for directions. The man frowns and says, "If I was trying to get to that village, I wouldn't start from here." If you're looking for your Element, you have to start where you are. You'll find your way as long as you tune in to your own true north and follow your energy. Many people started their lives moving down one path only to move in an entirely different direction later.

Moving Forward by Going Back

As a writer and speaker, I get all sorts of unexpected invitations. In 2011, I was the guest speaker at the hundredth anniversary meeting of the United States and Canadian Academy of Pathologists (USCAP) in San Antonio, Texas. I know nothing about pathology, by the way, and fortunately the organizers were aware of that. I was there to talk about innovation and creativity, which is as important in the field of pathology as in any other.

This was the largest gathering of physician pathologists in the world, with an attendance of almost four thousand professionals. My invitation to give a keynote to the conference as a non-professional in the field was unique in the history of the academy. It came about because the planning committee believed that creativity and discovering one's passion are essential to selecting and training pathologists for a future that we cannot imagine.

I was originally invited to speak to USCAP by Dr. Jeffrey Myers, a leader in the field of pathology. After first getting a degree in biology and qualifying as an MD, he held appointments at Washington University School of Medicine and the University of Alabama. He then went to the renowned Mayo Medical School where for two years he led a team effort to promote innovation, and then relocated to the University of Michigan in 2006 where he is now a leading member of its own Medical Innovation Center. He speaks around the world to specialist scientific and medical conferences, is a leading member of professional societies, has published widely in scholarly journals and has received numerous awards and honors for his outstanding work and contributions to his field.

Dr. Myers didn't have any of this in mind when he was in high school. As a teenager, a career in medicine in general and pathology in particular couldn't have been further from his mind. His passion was rock music and his plan was to be in a rock band. And for quite a while he was. He played guitar and sang, partly because it was what he loved to do and partly because it filled a vacuum in his life, which at that point had no other direction. He did well at school, but often felt disengaged from the whole process.

He told me that he was "hardly a 'rock star' but definitely a directionless kid who did well in school but whose heart and head were elsewhere. If you had said to any of my classmates or rock and roll peers that I'd someday be a Mayo Clinic doctor they would have laughed hilariously."

He eventually decided that he wasn't likely to make it in music and applied to study biology at college. He went on to a career in pathology that he loves and in which he's had an enormous impact.

"If I pause long enough to reflect on how the early knowledge of my calling in pathology expresses itself today, I see a rich blend of intimately associated experiences that keep me grounded in my Element. I discovered in my sixteen years at the Mayo Clinic that linking my passion for diagnostic pathology with opportunities in leadership and innovation is my moon shot! In 1992, I assumed a leadership post and served for ten years as Chair of Anatomic Pathology. It turned out to be a time during which I learned by making lots of mistakes. I was hotheaded and impatient. During that time I became a passionate advocate for patient safety and reducing errors in our discipline. Ultimately I calmed down and was able to change practice in ways that directly impacted the quality of the care and the service experience we offered to our providers and patients.

"After a decade I stepped down as Chair of Anatomic

Pathology and into a new role as Chair of the Innovation Work Group that was charged with 'expanding the culture and fostering an environment of clinical innovation at Mayo Clinic Rochester.' Being able to influence the future of my discipline, at least locally, is part of what keeps me in my Element. To some extent I'm always looking for the next big thing, unsatisfied with today's solutions. As long as I can combine diagnostic pathology with opportunities for continuous improvement, service excellence, and innovation in healthcare, I'm in!"

There's an interesting coda to Jeff Myers' story that was partly driven by our meeting in San Antonio. A few months after I spoke at the convention he went to a Jeff Beck concert. Shortly afterward he picked up a guitar for the first time in thirty-seven years. He realized that there was no reason not to return to the Element of his teenage years, and he drove to a regional guitar store and bought an Eric Clapton signature Stratocaster ("Blackie") and a Marshall amplifier. "An advantage of the path I chose," he told me, "is that I can now afford the guitars and equipment that were out of reach in my youth!" Together with two equally aged members of his department, he has laid the foundations of a band playing seventies and eighties rock/blues, including Cream, Lynyrd Skynyrd and the Allman Brothers. "For now we're calling ourselves Lost in Processing. I decided I no longer had to choose between medicine and music—perhaps I could do both. So far I'm learning that it doesn't detract from my career in medicine, while also discovering that I'm no better a musician than I was before!"

Jeffrey Myers' experience confirms that you may have more than one Element and love them both equally. It also shows that sometimes the next step forward is to retrace a path that you thought you'd left far behind you. As I say, life is not linear.

Follow Your Spirit

Whatever your circumstances, you always have options. As many of the stories here have shown, you may be in the most extreme circumstances, but you can always choose to think, feel and act differently. The critical factor is to make a move—to take the next step. To do that you need to look inward as well as outward. You need to tune in to your self and be open to where your spirit may be pointing.

One of the clearest ways of knowing that you are not in your Element is if your spirit is constantly heavy. This is how photographer Chris Jordan once felt. There was a time, when he was a corporate lawyer, when every day felt "like sitting down and doing pages of long division, which is something I dread." As soon as he started practicing law, he told me, "I had this horrible realization. I probably had it much earlier, but I wouldn't allow myself to go there."

The irony in Jordan's case is that he found what he was truly passionate about while in law school. Unfortunately, it wasn't the legal profession. Making a decision all too many make, he buried his desires so he could get his degree. "I had this whole series of false starts and failures up to then and I wanted to show myself and the people around me that I could stick with something. I chose the worst possible thing to stick with. I spent eleven years in a state of something very close to clinical depression as a corporate lawyer. From the very beginning it was totally unfulfilling to me. Not only did I feel I wasn't contributing anything to the world, but in many cases it was directly contrary to my principles."

Jordan's work life was miserable, but his life outside of work was becoming increasingly meaningful. He started exploring what he could do with large format cameras in the evenings and weekends, and he found himself more and more drawn to it. He placed some of his photos in his office, and his law firm hung some of his pictures in their conference rooms. "Every now and then, people would come into my office and say, 'Chris, why are you doing this? You could be having a kick-ass career as a photographer. Why are you a lawyer?' I would laugh as though they were joking because I was scared to take the risk."

Ultimately, though, Jordan realized that he was taking an even greater risk, one that finally pushed him out of the false comfort of quiet desperation. "As I got closer to forty, I began to fear not living my life. I feared becoming old and being filled with regret that I didn't take the risk of living. That fear, instead of being a wall in front of me, was like a giant cowboy boot kicking my ass from behind. The thing I realized was that if I didn't take the risk of living, I was guaranteed to fail. In the law firms I was working at I could see guys who had taken that route. They'd sit around having bitter conversations about how awful their lives were. I could hit the fast-forward button and see that I was headed there. I figured if I left the practice of law, I had at least a fifty-fifty chance."

Jordan left his firm at the end of 2002 with a commitment to succeed in the field of photography. To make sure that he couldn't go running back to law the first time things got difficult, he resigned from the Bar in January 2003. Living on his five-year-old son's college fund (assuming he would be able to replenish that fund long before his son needed it), he set out to make a career of his passion. This would not prove to be easy. Shooting with an eight-by-ten camera was extremely expensive—"$25 every time you click the shutter"—and other equipment costs were terribly high. The college fund was gone by the fall, Jordan's 401(k) didn't last much longer, and his wife's 401(k) money was gone by the summer of 2004. Certainly, someone more timid about making the most of his Element would have been seeking paralegal work or at the very least a part-time job at Starbucks by this point. Jordan, though, continued to believe that something was going to happen.

"I was pretty much on the mat and the referee had counted to two. But then I got a call from a gallery owner named Paul Kopeikin down in L.A. He said he'd seen my work and he wondered if I was going to be in L.A. anytime soon. I booked a flight that day." Kopeikin loved Jordan's photography and said he wanted to exhibit it the first chance he could. That turned out to be February 2005, which wouldn't have been a terribly long wait if Jordan weren't completely broke. The opportunity was too good to ignore, though, so Jordan and his wife signed up for a number of credit cards. "I just kept going. I knew I was going to have an audience for my work, so I really stepped it up. I flew all the way across the country to take one photograph of cell phones. By the time February came, we were something like $80,000 in credit card debt."

The break Jordan envisioned arrived with the gallery showing Kopeikin arranged. He sold enough photographs at that February event to pay off everything he owed the credit card companies. Then a New York gallery did a show that gave Jordan a bit of a financial cushion, though he sank most of that into a benefit series and book about the aftermath of Hurricane Katrina in New Orleans.

With the validation that came with the big sales and critical acclaim Jordan was now regularly receiving, he decided to follow his instincts and push his work in more ambitious directions. In the fall of 2006, he started on a series he called "Running the

Numbers." As Jordan describes it, "'Running the Numbers' looks at contemporary American culture through the austere lens of statistics. Each image portrays a specific quantity of something: fifteen million sheets of office paper (five minutes of paper use); 106,000 aluminum cans (thirty seconds of can consumption) and so on. My hope is that images representing these quantities might have a different effect than the raw numbers alone."

This work was entirely different from anything Jordan had ever done before and, to his consternation, his inner circle was not impressed. "The first few people who saw the images gave me horrible responses. One of my most trusted advisors said, 'This is not photography. It's certainly not art. It's a road to nowhere.'" Still, following a path that those who are truly in their Element so often follow, Jordan went with his gut. He released these photographs online and this was the first time his work went viral. In the spring of 2007, he was getting hundreds of thousands of hits on his website. He had to hire an assistant just to answer his e-mail. The series completely changed his profile as a photographer, reaching a far wider audience than he'd ever reached before.

"I've made it my practice to notice when I'm starting to feel comfortable doing a certain kind of work. That's when all the alarm bells go off and I realize it's time to strike off into territories unknown. I'm in that place again. My 'Running the Numbers' series is beginning to feel like my day job. I still want to do more because there are more issues I'd like to portray, but it doesn't feel like a creative risk anymore. One thing I've done is go to Midway Island to photograph dead baby albatrosses filled up with plastic. That's a creative risk—the art world isn't exactly clamoring for pictures of dead baby birds. When I put that art on my website, though, it went way more viral than any of my previous work."

Chris Jordan found his Element when he decided that risking

everything was better than the alternative. He stays in his Element by continuously pushing himself. It has led to a richly rewarding life, though not necessarily a comfortable one.

"There are a lot of anxieties that go along with this. If there's one thing I would say to someone who wants to take the risk of doing what they love, it would be to learn to bear anxiety." It's the price of allowing yourself to answer the question, "What's next?" But paying that price can lead to a completely different level of fulfillment.

As Chris Jordan's story shows, there can be risks in taking the high road to your Element. But there are other sorts of risks in ignoring the call of your spirit. If you know what your Element is, you can only ignore it by damping down the parts of you to which it appeals. The result can be a dull spiritual ache that holds you back where there should be an impulse of energy that drives you forward. Like Jeffrey Myers', Jordan's story illustrates the principle that your starting point does not determine your eventual course in life.

Exercise Fourteen: Your Initial Action Plan

If you've been keeping up with them by now you've accumulated materials, images, ideas and feelings from thirteen exercises and more than fifty questions throughout this book. It's impossible for me to know, of course, what stage you've reached in your own reflections on finding your Element. You may be completely clear by now about the direction you want to move in, and the place you want to get to. Equally, you may still be sorting through a range of possibilities and feel surer about some things than others. You may feel you have a clearer sense of your aptitudes than your passions, for example, or vice versa. Whatever stage you've reached, take some time to review all the exercises that you've done so far and to take stock of what you think you've discovered. To do this:

- Take one more large sheet of paper and draw four large circles on it. Draw them so that they all overlap in the center and create a common space. You may remember from elementary school that this is called a Venn diagram.
- Give each circle a name: aptitudes, passions, attitudes and opportunities.
- In each of the circles, write down four or five statements that express what you need to do next to deepen your understanding of that area of yourself. Make these statements as practical as possible.
- You should consider seriously taking all of these actions over time. But what do you do first?
- Look at all of these statements carefully and spend as much time as you like reflecting on them. When you're ready, put them in order of priority. You can give them a number or color code them, whatever works.
- When you're happy with the priorities, write the top priority from each circle in the center part where each of the circles overlaps.
- Consider these four steps as your initial action plan.
- Remember, you can't plan the whole journey—just the next steps.

One important reason for keeping your options open is that you're not limited to one Element for life. Some people find they love several things equally; others that their passions shift and evolve. Finding your Element for now doesn't mean that you're locked in to it forever. In fact, when you ask, "What's next?" the question can easily become, "What else?"

What Else?

Earlier in the book, we talked about David Ogilvy's dramatic transition from farmer to ad-man. There are many others. Martha Stewart, for example, began her career as a model, a job she took to pay for the part of the tuition to Barnard College (where she was studying art, European history and architectural history) not covered by her scholarship. She continued modeling after graduation, appearing in print and television ads for Breck shampoo, Clairol and even Tareyton cigarettes. Her skills as a lifestyle guru didn't come to the fore until she moved to Westport, Connecticut, with her husband many years later and renovated the 1805 farmhouse they'd bought there. This led her to a catering business that capitalized on her love for food and then to a series of books combining the two that served as the springboard for the lifestyle empire she now oversees.

Janet Robinson (no relation) was a public school teacher in New England when she decided to move into the business world, taking a sales management position with The New York Times Company. While she may have been an extremely dynamic teacher, her skills outside of the classroom have also proven to be considerable. She moved from sales management to senior vice president for the advertising sales and marketing unit of The New York Times Company Women's Magazine Group to President and General Manager of the *New York Times* newspaper, and now serves as President and Chief Executive Officer of The New York Times Company. She is regularly ranked as one of the most powerful women in media, and she's still teaching people a thing or two.

Unlike Jeffrey Myers, Taryn Rose had a career in medicine mapped out from the time she was young. Her father actually was a pathologist and it was generally assumed that she was going to follow his path. She went to USC Medical School and completed her residency as an orthopedic surgeon. The long days on her feet while wearing heels, and the multitude of female patients she'd seen whose maladies were related to the shoes they were wearing, led her to an epiphany: there had to be a way to make shoes that both looked good and felt good—and she was the right person to figure this out.

Over the next three years, she worked on the business plan for her eponymous shoe company, one that quickly became a prestigious and hugely popular label. *Fast Company* magazine named her number one among "25 Women Entrepreneurs Who Are Changing the Game." There were no other orthopedic surgeons on the list.

Breaking Your Mold

The fact is that we all have a tendency to categorize and label each other, by age, accent, appearance, gender, ethnicity and especially occupation. When people meet socially the most common question they ask is, "What do you do?" and then they adjust their attitude to you accordingly. We can easily typecast ourselves in the same ways. The reason I resist suggesting particular "types" of people in this book is that there is rarely a complete fit with any given individual. Even so, people tend to play into them once the label has been applied, as with the Barnum effect.

A business consultancy I know in the United States has a successful process for enabling groups from different companies to work together on priorities and strategies. One feature of their process is that members of the groups don't wear job labels. You could be working with the CEO of another company, or the head of finance, or with a junior salesperson, and you wouldn't know. The reason is to focus the group on the qualities of each other's contributions rather than on their roles or status.

Exercise Fifteen: Letter to a Supporter

With that in mind, try this exercise:

Imagine you are not you but someone who has met you and has spent time getting to know your interests, attitudes, hopes and aspirations. Imagine that person is writing about you to someone else who is interested in supporting your future plans. This person has no preconceptions about who you are but would like to know more.

Write about yourself in the third person: i.e., "Ken (or whatever your name really is) particularly enjoys . . ." Don't mention your age, gender, ethnicity, social background or current situation. Do mention your interests, capabilities and aspirations and what you feel you have to learn and would like to experience next. Describe your personal qualities, the achievements you value most and the opportunities you hope to have in the future.

Write the letter as quickly as you can, using the techniques of morning pages and automatic writing. Make as many points as you want. Don't worry about editing it. As you do this, look back at your SWOT analysis in chapter seven for ideas and inspiration. Remember to write as someone else might see you who doesn't have the preconceptions that close friends, family or people you currently work with might have of you. Try to see yourself fresh as someone else might.

When you've finished the letter, read it through and make a list of the main points you've made. Use them to create a mind map of steps you would like to take now to learn more about your interests and aptitudes and the next part of your own journey. Look at each of them and ask yourself how you can make them happen.

When "Next" Is the Only Option

Often, one of the most significant reasons for avoiding finding out "what's next" is that you don't need to. What you're doing right now might not be lighting up your life, but it's good enough. More important, it's safe—you're getting a good income from it, your peers respect you, the community defines you as successful. The impetus simply isn't there, as much as you'd love to find out if you could make it knitting scarves, running a spa or teaching English as a second language. If your world were turned upside down . . . maybe. But things are good. Why mess with them?

Perhaps there's something to be learned from those whose worlds *were* turned upside down. Mark Frankland, for example, might never have discovered his true passion if he hadn't suddenly found himself without a job. Mark had once written a song for his wife that included the African proverb, "Life is like eating an elephant; you need to do it one mouthful at a time." He didn't realize it at the time, but this lyric captured the essence of his search for his Element.

"I think that part of the process of overcoming a big hurdle," he said to me, "is not looking at how big the problem is, but just trying to find out the next step you should take. Sometimes it's drastic, and sometimes it's very little. Sometimes a little thing can make massive changes to your life."

Music had a key place in Mark's world from a very young age. Unfortunately, so did the big hurdles. "I was always singing. When I was on the stage I always found myself in a singing part. When I was in primary school there was a competition called the Muir Cup. Each year, the silver and the gold medals would go to the people in the grade in front of me. Then, in my last year of primary school, it was my year to get the gold, because I'd won the bronze the year before and the two people ahead of me had moved up to secondary school. Then my teacher decided to discipline me for not doing my homework or something and didn't allow me to go into the competition. I still remember it as quite a significant moment in my life."

Another complication was that Mark came from a broken home. He found himself endlessly seeking his father's approval, and this included his choice of careers, which took him far away from making music.

"I spent several years trying to pursue a career that my father would be proud of. He's a surveyor and he was building private hospitals up and down the country. I tried to find a career that would have a tick of approval from the old man. I was just trying to be the good boy, but I wasn't the good happy boy.

"I went into all different occupations. The last thing I did was television production, which most people would think of as a really exciting job. When I was doing the creative side of the business, it was good, but very quickly the finances of the company I was working for declined to the point where they weren't going to make programs anymore, and I went into sales. I did it for eight years because it was good money, and by this point, I had a wife, kid, dog—the whole thing. It seemed like a good niche for me to be in, but there's always that kind of nagging disappointment in the back of your mind. I didn't have a sense of purpose. When the situation at work came to the point where I began to lose myself, I was faced with the options of staying in a job I wasn't enjoying or finding alternative employment in the same industry. Neither one floated my boat."

Then the options became even more limited, as it became clear that Mark's job was about to be cut.

"Things started to slowly unravel, but I had started to sing again. When I was drunk, I'd sing a song at the local pub about a garden gnome. That was the extent of my musical career. But I always used to write songs for my families for their weddings and bar mitzvahs. I would happily perform sober in front of my family, but not in front of a crowd I didn't know. I wrote a song for my sister's fortieth birthday and sang it at her birthday party, which meant that I had to sing in front of some of my peers. They all responded very favorably to the song. Later on, when I'd gone to an open mike night and I was drinking my way to the garden gnome song, someone said, 'Why don't you sing that song about your sister?' When the situation with work started to go wrong, I remembered that I'd spent my youth dissecting records. Now I thought I'd see if I could try to pursue that a bit further.

"My wife suggested that instead of going to evening classes in music production, that I should take a degree. I live about twenty miles south of London, and locally there's The Academy of Contemporary Music, which is billed as Europe's leading rock school. I took my fourteen-year-old daughter with me as backup when I went to take a look around the school. That's when I discovered that they had a business school there as well. There was a bit of happenstance about it, but you have to make your own luck."

Thrown into this environment because the work he'd been relying on was no longer available, Mark found the inspiration he'd been lacking for most of his professional life. He was facing an enormous challenge at a critical point in his life—much like facing the prospect of eating an elephant—but because he was doing something that mattered to him so much, he found the drive, determination and attitude to accomplish it. He matriculated in school full-time with the complete support of his wife—which was critical, since paying the mortgage was going to be a lot tougher than it had been when he had his sales job—and he came away with a degree in both the creative and business ends of the music industry. His final dissertation gave him his clearest sense of direction yet.

"My dissertation was about why creativity and believing that you could be anybody you wanted to be was so prevalent in the primary schools and how they slowly work it out of you. The next opportunity you have of fulfilling some of your hobbies full-time is when you retire. I couldn't figure out why that was. I knew, looking at the lines and lines of people who would queue up to be on "The X Factor" and "Britain's Got Talent" that there was an appetite among people to find a sense of purpose."

This inspired Mark to found Good Gracious Music, a label dedicated to helping people fulfill latent dreams of recording and releasing songs. "I set up my company to try to encourage people that you didn't have to become a rock superstar to enjoy making music and releasing albums, especially in today's self-publishing Internet world. Good Gracious Music is now focused on finding people over the age of thirty who used to be in a band when they were kids and getting them back into the studio and back into writing."

When he was younger, Mark didn't have the disposition to try to make it in the music business. He let his sense of obligation to others overwhelm his desire to explore his greatest passion. Faced with unemployment and the loss of his safety net, though, he decided the time was right to make a meal of the elephant. His wife lent her financial acumen to make sure they could pay the bills, and he found support from everyone in his family—including his father, who Mark had tried to please for so long by staying away from music.

Many years after a teacher took away his dream of turning music into gold, Mark Frankland is making a living in the field he loves. Good Gracious Music is now in its fourth year and is growing annually. Yet if things had been just a little bit better in his old job, he might have never done the thing he was meant to do.

I think there might be a message here for all of us. While there are often risks associated with moving from your current pursuit to one that more closely aligns to your passions, very few enterprises come without risk these days. The Chinese refer to a job that you're guaranteed to have for life as an "iron rice bowl." But how many of these really exist, especially in an era of global economic uncertainty?

At the same time, I regularly hear stories of people like Mark Frankland who, when suddenly finding themselves out of "safe" jobs, discover a way to navigate through the financial uncertainty to create something new and significant for themselves.

While I would never advocate your giving up any sense of security, if you feel that what's next for you might be much more satisfying than what you have now, maybe you should consider a leap and trust the safety net will appear. It's a bit like the philosophy of living every day as though it were your last. This is, of course, a ridiculous argument. If I were living every day as though it were my last, my lifestyle would probably hasten the arrival of my true last day. Even so, necessity can generate unexpected creativity. It can give you just the push you need, not only to ask, but also to answer the question, "What's next?"

The Malleable Mammal

In chapter two, I suggested one way in which human beings are distinctly different from the rest of life on earth. Here's another that you might not have considered. We are virtually alone among mammals at coming into the world when we're simply not ready to deal with it. We've all seen images of foals, just hours after being born, standing on toothpick legs and galloping around. Puppies seem bent on chewing up the furniture (and getting their close-ups on YouTube) from the moment they leave the womb. On the other hand, newborn human babies don't do much of anything. We may gaze on them in wonder, but this is decidedly a one-way interaction. Most significantly, left on their own, most newborns wouldn't survive more than a couple of days.

"In many ways, your new baby is more a fetus than an infant," Dr. Harvey Karp says in his book, *The Happiest Baby on the Block*. "Had you delayed your delivery just three more months, your baby would have been born with the ability to smile, coo and flirt. (Who wouldn't want that on their baby's first day of life!)"

Dr. Karp realizes, of course, that delaying delivery three months is a physical impossibility. He is, after all, a doctor. He's come to believe strongly, though, that all babies, and especially those who suffer from colic, would benefit from a "fourth trimester" in a situation that resembles the womb as closely as possible. To ease the transition from the uterus to the outside world, he recommends five procedures that activate the "calming reflex"—swaddling, shushing, swinging, laying babies down on their sides and allowing them to suck. Millions of parents have embraced Dr. Karp's advice and have used it to ease the path for their children—and themselves.

This fourth trimester concept is a powerful metaphor for living our lives in an optimal way. Just as a baby is not really "done" when it comes from its mother's womb, none of us have finished the act of growing and evolving even as we head toward physical maturity. No matter how in the zone you might feel yourself to be right now, there's a good chance that your best and most rewarding work is still ahead of you.

Consider Gandhi. As a lawyer, he'd been doing very good work championing civil disobedience for many years. But he didn't have a real effect on India and the rest of the world until he was sixty-one and led a two-hundred-and-forty-mile march to protest British rule of his country.

Consider Frank McCourt. He had an accomplished career as a teacher that extended for decades. It was only when he was in his sixties that McCourt became known to the world as the bestselling author of *Angela's Ashes*.

Civic Ventures is a "think tank on boomers, work and social purpose." Recognizing that people who have already had long careers are capable of contributing so much more, Civic Ventures has launched a series of programs to demonstrate "the value of experience in solving serious social problems." Among these are their website, encore.org, which compiles resources, connections and an inspiring collection of personal stories; a college initiative for retraining boomers for new careers; and fellowships that place experienced professionals in short-term assignments with social-purpose organizations.

One of their most significant programs is the Civic Ventures' Purpose Prize, a $100,000 award given to five winners annually who are over sixty and "changing the world." One of the 2011 winners was Randal Charlton. Charlton has seemingly embraced the notion of following his inspirations wherever they might take him. He's been a life sciences journalist, he's tended dairy cows for a Saudi sheik, he started a jazz club, and he's founded several companies. One of these companies had a wildly successful IPO, which allowed Charlton to retire. The only problem was that he found retirement boring. "I wasn't ready to play golf or shuffleboard," he told me. "My game wasn't good enough. I felt that I needed a purpose."

Rather than finding that purpose in a quiet hobby, Charlton decided to visit the president of Wayne State University in Detroit to ask if the school might have any use for him. As it turned out, the president felt there was a spot that would benefit greatly from someone with Charlton's varied skill set. Soon, he was executive director of TechTown, a business incubator in midtown Detroit, charged with the mission of helping to turn around the city's devastated economy. Randal pointed out that, in spite of his wide range of business experience, he had very little that qualified him for such a position. "Never mind," the president said to him, "you'll learn."

Randal not only learned, he thrived—and in the process found a powerful sense of inspiration. "It was probably one of the most rewarding jobs of my career. I'd made lots of mistakes over the course of my career—everyone does. Being able to pass along the benefit of those mistakes to younger entrepreneurs was exciting and very rewarding. On top of that, I was in Detroit where there was an economic meltdown in progress. Here was a city where any new business was celebrated like winning the Super Bowl. It was a tremendous feeling of accomplishment."

"Detroit had twenty percent unemployment and another big percentage of underemployment, as well as racial problems and—on top of all that—the near collapse of the auto industry. All of which demands that we create a more entrepreneurial culture here in Detroit, and we at TechTown are at the epicenter of that."

The TechTown Charlton inherited was light on participants and even lighter on resources. Today, the TechTown building has two hundred and fifty tenants, and TechTown has trained thousands of entrepreneurs and helped its clients raise more than fourteen million dollars. TechTown has been an important player in Detroit's reemergence, and it has served as a model for other entrepreneurial incubators that have subsequently entered the scene.

"I found it very rewarding having to challenge myself late in my career. Once you start to get too comfortable with a job, watch out, because you might be freewheeling and not all using all of your mental and physical assets to your best advantage."

As all of these examples show, your life doesn't have to play on a single track. You're not limited to one Element for life. Some people find they love several things equally: others that their passions shift and evolve. Finding your Element for now doesn't mean that you're locked into it forever. Your life can be multifaceted, evolutionary, and in a process of constant growth and possibility.

Some Questions

- What experiences would you like to have that you haven't had yet?
- Are there things that you loved doing in the past that you would love to try again now?
- What's stopping you?
- If you couldn't fail, what would you most like to achieve?
- How could you adjust to a change in financial circumstances?
- What resources could you fall back on if absolutely necessary?
- What's next?

CHAPTER TEN

Living a Life of Passion and Purpose

I ASKED AT the beginning of this book how many people have ever lived. I said that as far as anyone can estimate, there might have been around eighty to one hundred and ten billion of us. And yet each of us is unique and every life is different. The gift of being human is that we have deep creative resources and from these we can continuously transform our lives if we choose. Whether you aim to change the whole world or the world within you, the limits are set as much by your imagination as by your current circumstances. This has been true for all people since the beginnings of human history.

Your own quest has never been taken before. But the nature of life's journey is as ancient as humanity itself. Writers and philosophers down through the ages have pointed to the same principles, and they lie at the heart of all the great myths and stories of human adventure and achievement. Identifying these principles was at the heart of Joseph Campbell's writings on the Hero's Journey. As Campbell puts it, "A good life is one hero journey after another. Over and over again, you are called to the realm of adventure. You are called to new horizons. Each time, there is the same problem: do I dare? And then, if you do dare, the dangers are there, and the help also, and the fulfillment or the fiasco. There's always the possibility of a fiasco. But there's also the possibility of bliss."

All quests involve risks and you can't anticipate them all. They involve opportunities too and you can't foresee all of those, either. You can only set a direction and take the first steps. You then need to stay open to risks and to possibilities and be willing to respond to both. This is how the creative process works and how organic processes take their shape. Martin Luther King had just this in mind when he said, "Take the first step in faith. You don't have to see the whole staircase, just take the first step."

Although you can't predict the future, it pays to look ahead. How long do you think your journey may be? Fortunately, we normally don't know. But if all goes well, you may live for eighty, ninety or maybe a hundred years. That may seem a long time if you're currently bored or frustrated with your life. But in cosmic terms, it's less than a heartbeat. Do you hope to enjoy your life or just endure it? Some people resent getting old, of course, and it does have its challenges. As the actress Bette Davis put it, "Getting old is not for the faint hearted." Even so, as the old proverb says, "Don't regret becoming old: it's a privilege denied to many." And it is.

Someone once said that whenever you see the dates of someone's life the most important part is the dash in the middle. What did they do to fill the dash? It's a good question to ask yourself. There are some important lessons to be learned from people who are at the end of their journey and know it.

Bronnie Ware is a writer who worked for many years in palliative care. Her patients suffered from incurable conditions and knew they were dying. She took care of them during the last three to twelve weeks of their lives. People grow a lot, she says, when they are faced with their own mortality. "I learnt never to under-estimate someone's capacity for growth. Some changes were phe-nomenal. Each experienced a variety of emotions, as expected, denial, fear, anger, remorse, more denial and eventually acceptance. Every single patient found their peace before they departed, though, every one of them."

When she asked her patients whether they had any regrets in their lives or if they would have done anything differently, a number of themes came up again and again. These are the most common ones:

I WISH I'D HAD THE COURAGE TO LIVE A LIFE TRUE TO MYSELF, NOT THE LIFE OTHERS EXPECTED OF ME.

This was the most common regret of all. When people realize that their life is almost over and look back on it, they often realize how many of their dreams have been unfulfilled. "Most people had not honored even a half of their dreams and had to die know-ing that it was due to choices they had made, or not made."

I WISH I HADN'T WORKED SO HARD.

This came from every male patient that she nursed. They missed their children's youth and their partner's companionship. Women also spoke of this regret. But as most were from an older genera-tion, many of the female patients had not been breadwinners. "All of the men deeply regretted spending so much of their lives on the treadmill of work."

I WISH I'D HAD THE COURAGE TO EXPRESS MY FEELINGS.

Many people suppressed their feelings to keep peace with others. As a result, they settled for a life they didn't want and never became who they could have been. "Many developed illnesses relating to the bitterness and resentment they carried as a result."

I WISH I'D STAYED IN TOUCH WITH MY FRIENDS.

Many people didn't appreciate the full benefits of old friends until their dying weeks and it was not always possible to track them down. Many had become so caught up in their own lives that they had let golden friendships slip by over the years. "There were many deep regrets about not giving friendships the time and effort that they deserved. Everyone misses their friends when they are dying."

I WISH THAT I HAD LET MYSELF BE HAPPIER.

Many people didn't realize until the end that happiness is a choice. They had stayed stuck in old patterns and habits. "The so-called 'comfort' of familiarity overflowed into their emotions, as well as their physical lives. Fear of change had them pretending to others, and to their selves, that they were content, when deep within, they longed to laugh properly and have silliness in their life again."

Bronnie Ware's experience with terminal patients suggests some simple but important lessons for those with much of their lives still ahead of them. Here are some of them:

HONOR YOUR DREAMS

It's important to try and honor at least some of your dreams along the way. Take the opportunities you have, especially when your health is good. Health brings a freedom very few realize, until they no longer have it.

REDUCE THE BURDEN

By simplifying your lifestyle and making conscious choices along the way, it is possible to reduce what you think you need to earn and have to live a fulfilling life. By creating more space and time in your life, you may find that you become happier and more open to new opportunities.

VALUE YOUR OWN LIFE AND FEELINGS

You can't control the reactions of others. Although people may initially react badly when you speak honestly about your feelings, in the end it raises the relationship to a new and healthier level. Either that or it releases the unhealthy relationship from your life. Either way, you win.

VALUE THOSE YOU LOVE

When people are facing their approaching death, they want to get their financial affairs in order if possible, usually for the benefit of those they love. But in the final reckoning, it's not money or status that really matters. In the final weeks, it all comes down to love and relationships. That's all that remains in the end.

I suggested in chapter one that navigating your life is like being on the open seas. You can cling close to the known shores or your can set a more exploratory course. Mark Twain used the same metaphor. Reflecting on his own life and achievements he had this advice: "Twenty years from now you will be more disappointed by the things that you didn't do than by the ones you did do. So throw off the bowlines. Sail away from the safe harbor. Catch the trade winds in your sails. Explore. Dream. Discover."

We're all shaped to some degree by our own biographies and cultures and it's easy to believe that what's happened before determines what has to come next. The American poet Ralph Waldo Emerson thought otherwise. "What lies behind us," he wrote, "and what lies before us are tiny matters compared to what lies within us."

Finding your Element is about discovering what lies within you and, in doing so, transforming what lies before you. "Risk" is a short poem often attributed to the writer Anais Nin. It uses a powerful, organic metaphor to contrast the risks of suppressing your potential with the rewards of releasing it:

> *And then the day came,*
> *when the risk*
> *to remain tight*
> *in a bud*
> *was more painful*
> *than the risk*
> *it took*
> *to blossom.*

Like the rest of nature, human talents and passions are tremendously diverse and they take many forms. As individuals, we're all motivated by different dreams and we thrive—and we wilt too—in very different circumstances. Recognizing your own dreams and the conditions you need to fulfill them are essential to becoming who you can be. Finding your own Element won't guarantee that you'll spend the rest of your life in a constant, unbroken state of pleasure and delight. It will give you a deeper sense of who you really are and of the life you could and maybe should live.

Notes

Introduction

"The Forer Effect," *The Skeptic's Dictionary*, February 10, 2012, http://www.skepdic.com/forer.html.

Jerome K. Jerome, *Three Men in a Boat; to Say Nothing of the Dog!* (New York: Time, 1964).

Chapter One: Finding Your Element

Tony Buzan and Barry Buzan, *The Mind Map Book: How to Use Radiant Thinking to Maximize Your Brain's Untapped Potential* (New York: Plume, 1993).

M. G. Siegler, "Eric Schmidt: Every 2 Days We Create as Much Information as We Did Up to 2003," *TechCrunch*, accessed July 4, 2012, http://techcrunch.com/2010/08/04/schmidt-data/.

D. Evans and R. Hutley, "The Explosion of Data: How to Make Better Business Decisions by Turning 'Infolution' Into Knowledge," Cisco.com N.p., n.d., http://www.cisco.com/web/about/ac79/docs/pov/Data_Explosion_IBSG.pdf.

Eckhart Tolle, *The Power of Now: A Guide to Spiritual Enlightenment* (Novato, CA: New World Library, 1999).

"How Many People Can Live on Planet Earth?" Top Documentary Films, February 8, 2012, http://topdocumentaryfilms.com/how-many-people-can-live-on-planet-earth/.

Judith Butler, *Precarious Life: The Powers of Mourning and Violence* (London: Verso, 2004).

George Kelly, *A Theory of Personality; The Psychology of Personal Constructs,* (New York: W. W. Norton, 1963).

Vivek Wadhwa, "Silicon Valley Needs Humanities Students," *Washington Post,* May 18, 2012; accessed July 04, 2012, http://www.washington post.com/national/on-innovations/why-you-should-quit-your-tech-job-and-study-the-humanities/2012/05/16/gIQAvibbUU_story.html.

Anne Fisher, "Finding a Dream Job: A Little Chaos Theory Helps," Time Business, March 4, 2009; accessed December 30, 2011, http://www.time.com/time/business/article/0,8599,1882369,00.html.

Katharine Brooks, *You Majored in What? Mapping Your Path From Chaos to Career* (New York, NY: Viking, 2009).

Julia Cameron, *The Artist's Way: A Spiritual Path to Higher Creativity* (Los Angeles, CA: Jeremy P. Tarcher/Perigee, 1992).

Chapter Two: What Are You Good At?

"El Sistema: Social Support and Advocacy Through Musical Education," Distributed Intelligence, October 11, 2011, video.mit.edu/watch/el-sistema-social-support-2nd-advocacy-through-musical-education-9553/.

Charlotte Higgins, "How Classical Music Is Helping Venezuelan Children Escape Poverty," The Guardian Music, accessed October 11, 2011, http://www.guardian.co.uk/music/2006/nov/24/classicalmusicandopera.

"Venezuela—El Sistema USA," El Sistema USA, accessed October 11, 2011, http://elsistemausa.org/el-sistema/venezuela/.

Daniel J. Wakin, "Los Angeles Orchestra to Lead Youth Effort," *The New York Times,* accessed October 11, 2011, www.nytimes.com/2011/10/05/arts/music/los-angeles-philharmonic-to-lead-a-sistema-style-project.html.

"Jose Antonio Abreu," TED Profile, ted.com, accessed October 11, 2011, http://www.ted.com/speakers/jose_antonio_abreu.html.

Jon Henley, "Jamie Oliver's Fifteen: A Winning Recipe," The Guardian News and Media, April 9, 2012, accessed June 7, 2012, http://www.guardian.co.uk/society/2012/apr/09/jamie-oliver-fifteen-winning-recipe.

"Jamie Roberts," Fifteen Cornwall, June 8, 2012, http://www.fifteencornwall.co.uk/apprentice-chefs/Jamie%20Roberts. pdf.

"About StrengthsFinder 2.0," Strengths home page, accessed September 30, 2011, http://strengths.gallup.com/110440/about-strengthsfinder-2 .aspx.

"CareerScope® V10 | VRI," Vocational Research Institute, accessed September 30, 2011, http://www.vri.org/products/careerscope-v10/benefits.

"General Aptitude Test Battery," Career Choice Guide, accessed September 30, 2011, http://www.careerchoiceguide.com/general-aptitude-test -battery.html.

"Ability Profiler (AP)," O*NET Resource Center, accessed September 30, 2011, http://www.onetcenter.org/AP.html.

"Blazing a Trail," Financial Times Ltd. Asia Africa Intelligence Wire, 2005, accessed October 11, 2011. http://www.accessmylibrary.com.

Chapter Three: How Do You Know?

"The Story of Sam," Learning Beyond Schooling June 1, 2012, http:// learningbeyondschooling.org/2011/05/21/the-story-of-sam-dancing/.

"David A. Kolb on Experiential Learning," Informal Education home page, accessed December 22, 2010, http://www.infed.org/biblio/ b-explrn.htm.

"Learning Styles," North Carolina State WWW4 Server, accessed December 22, 2010, http://www4.ncsu.edu/unity/lockers/users/f/felder/ public/Learning_Styles.html.

VARK—A Guide to Learning Styles, accessed December 22, 2010, http:// www.vark-learn.com/english/index.asp.

Centers for Disease Control and Prevention, December 12, 2011, accessed July 4, 2012, http://www.cdc.gov/ncbddd/adhd/prevalence.html.

Gardiner Harris, "F.D.A. Is Finding Attention Drugs in Short Supply," *The New York Times*, January 1, 2012, accessed July 4, 2012, http:// www.nytimes.com/2012/01/01/health/policy/fda-is-finding-attention -drugs-in-short-supply.html?pagewanted=all.

Chapter Four: What Do You Love?

Brian Norris, "What Is Passion?" briannorris.com, accessed January 27, 2012, http://www.briannorris.com/passion/what-is-passion.html.

George Washington Institute for Spirituality and Health, George Washington University, accessed January 27, 2012, http://www.gwumc.edu/gwish/aboutus/index.cfm.

George E. Vaillant, *Spiritual Evolution: A Scientific Defense of Faith* (New York: Broadway, 2008).

Abhijit Naik, "Interesting Facts about Nervous System," Buzzle Web Portal: Intelligent Life on the Web, October 10, 2011, accessed January 27, 2012, http://www.buzzle.com/articles/interesting-facts-about-nervous-system.html.

Susan L. Smalley, and Diana Winston. *Fully Present: The Science, Art, and Practice of Mindfulness.* (Cambridge, Mass: Da Capo Lifelong, 2010).

The Joseph Campbell Foundation home page, accessed November 17, 2011, http://www.jcf.org/new/index.php?categoryid=31.

Thérèse, *India's Summer* (Stamford, CT: Fiction Studio, 2012).

Chapter Five: What Makes You Happy?

Dan Baker and Cameron Stauth, *What Happy People Know: How the New Science of Happiness Can Change Your Life for the Better* (Emmaus, PA: Rodale, 2003).

David Rock, "New Study Shows Humans Are on Autopilot Nearly Half the Time," *Psychology Today*, November 14, 2011, accessed December 20, 2011, http://www.psychologytoday.com/blog/your-brain-work/201011/new-study-shows-humans-are-autopilot-nearly-half-the-time.

"Current Worldwide Suicide Rate," ChartsBin.com, accessed December 30, 2011, http://chartsbin.com/view/prm.

Andrew Weil, *Spontaneous Happiness* (New York: Little, Brown, 2011).

"Martin Seligman—Biography," University of Pennsylvania Positive Psychology Center, January 27, 2012, http://www.ppc.sas.upenn.edu/bio.htm.

Viktor E. Frankl, *Man's Search for Meaning* (Boston: Beacon, 2006).

Martin E. P. Seligman, *Authentic Happiness: Using the New Positive Psychology to Realize Your Potential for Lasting Fulfillment* (New York: Free Press, 2002).

"World Database of Happiness," Erasmus University, Rotterdam, accessed February 9, 2012, http://www1.eur.nl/fsw/happiness/.

Sonja Lyubomirsky, *The How of Happiness: A New Approach to Getting the Life You Want* (New York: Penguin, 2008).

Matthieu Ricard, *Happiness: A Guide to Developing Life's Most Important Skill*, Introduction, (New York: Little, Brown, 2007).

Robert Chalmers, "Matthieu Ricard: Meet Mr Happy," The Independent Profiles—People, November 22, 2011, http://www.independent .co.uk/news/people/profiles/matthieu-ricard-meet-mr-happy-436652 .html.

Gretchen Rubin, *The Happiness Project: Or, Why I Spent a Year Trying to Sing in the Morning, Clean My Closets, Fight Right, Read Aristotle, and Generally Have More Fun* (New York: Harper, 2011).

Gretchen Rubin, "How to Be Happier—in Four Easy Lessons," The Happiness Project, accessed November 22, 2011, http://www.happiness-project .com/happiness_project/2009/07/how-to-be-happier-in-four-easy -lessons.html.

Indra Nooyi, "Indra Nooyi's Mantras for Success," Rediff News, November 29, 2011, http://www.rediff.com/money/2008/sep/12sld4.htm.

Daniel Todd Gilbert, *Stumbling on Happiness* (New York: Vintage, 2007).

"Indra Nooyi's Graduation Remarks," businessweek.com, accessed November 29, 2011, http://www.businessweek.com/bwdaily/dnflash/ may2005/nf20050520_9852.htm.

Free the Children home page, accessed November 30, 2011, http://www .freethechildren.com/.

"Inspirational Kids: Craig Kielburger," EcoKids Online, November 30, 2011, http://www.ecokids.ca/pub/eco_info/topics/kids/craig.cfm.

Jerrilyn Jacobs, "The My Hero Project—Craig Kielburger," The My Hero Project, accessed November 30, 2011, http://myhero.com/go/hero.asp? hero=c_Kielburger.

Tracy Rysavy, "Free the Children: The Story of Craig Kielburger," YES! Magazine, accessed November 30, 2011, http://www.yesmagazine.org/ issues/power-of-one/free-the-children-the-story-of-craig-kielburger.

Chapter Six: What's Your Attitude?

"About Me," Enjoy Feet Massage and Jewellery, accessed July 2, 2012, http://www.enjoyfeet.co.uk/sue_kent.html.

Carol S. Dweck, *Mindset: The New Psychology of Success* (New York: Random House, 2006).

Kathy Kolbe, kolbe.com home page, accessed July 4, 2012, http://www.kolbe.com/.

"Better Results Through Better Thinking," Herrmann International, accessed July 4, 2012, www.hbdi.com/uploads/100029_practitionersarea/100608.pdf.

"Personality Type!" accessed February 10, 2012, http://www.personalitytype.com/.

Personality and Individual Differences Journal home page, Elsevier, accessed February 10, 2012, http://www.journals.elsevier.com/personality-and-individual-differences/.

"Test Your Optimism (Life Orientation Test)," EHLT, accessed February 10, 2012, http://ehlt.flinders.edu.au/education/DLiT/2006/helpinghands/LOTtest.pdf.

William Grimes, "Mimi Weddell, Model, Actress and Hat Devotee, Is Dead at 94," *The New York Times*, accessed February 14, 2012, http://www.nytimes.com/2009/10/06/movies/06weddell.html.

Hats Off (2008), The Internet Movie Database (IMDb), accessed February 14, 2012, http://www.imdb.com/title/tt1194127/.

Dennis McLellan, "Mimi Weddell Dies at 94; the Subject of 'Hats Off,'" *Los Angeles Times*, accessed February 14, 2012, http://www.latimes.com/news/obituaries/la-me-mimi-weddell4-2009oct04,0,7336710.story.

Chapter Seven: Where Are You Now?

Ben Strickland "Education Is Not Always Linear, Student Argues," oklahomadaily.com, February 1, 2012, accessed August 3, 2012, http://www.oudaily.com/news/2012/feb/01/college-education-isnt/.

Chapter Eight: Where's Your Tribe?

Jeffrey S. Minnich, "Plant Buddies—Plants That Grow Better When Next to Each Other," CBS Interactive Business Network, April 1, 1994, accessed July 2, 2012, http://www.accessmylibrary.com/article-1G1-14988868/plant-buddies-plants-grow.html

"Claus Meyer: Manifesto," Claus Meyer: Forside, January 11, 2012, http://www.clausmeyer.dk/en/the_new_nordic_cuisine_/manifesto_.html.

Julia Moskin, "New Nordic Cuisine Draws Disciples" *The New York Times*, August 23, 2011, accessed January 11, 2012, http://www.nytimes.com/2011/08/24/dining/new-nordic-cuisine-draws-disciples.html.

Chapter Nine: What's Next?

Harvey Karp, *The Happiest Baby on the Block: The New Way to Calm Crying and Help Your Newborn Baby Sleep Longer* (New York, NY: Bantam, 2002).

"Success After the Age of 60," Google Answers, accessed January 24, 2012, http://answers.google.com/answers/threadview?id=308654.

"About Civic Ventures Programs," Encore Careers, accessed January 24, 2012, http://www.encore.org/learn/aboutprograms.

"Randal Charlton," Encore Careers, January 24, 2012, http://www.encore.org/randal-charlton-0.

Chapter Ten: Living a Life of Passion and Purpose

Bronnie Ware, *The Top Five Regrets of the Dying: A Life Transformed by the Dearly Departing* (Carlsbad, CA: Hay House, 2012).

Index

ALLEN LANE

an imprint of

PENGUIN BOOKS

Recently Published

Paul Collier, *Exodus: Immigration and Multiculturalism in the 21st Century*

John Eliot Gardiner, *Music in the Castle of Heaven: Immigration and Multiculturalism in the 21st Century*

Catherine Merridale, *Red Fortress: The Secret Heart of Russia's History*

Ramachandra Guha, *Gandhi Before India*

Vic Gatrell, *The First Bohemians: Life and Art in London's Golden Age*

Richard Overy, *The Bombing War: Europe 1939-1945*

Charles Townshend, *The Republic: The Fight for Irish Independence, 1918-1923*

Eric Schlosser, *Command and Control*

Sudhir Venkatesh, *Floating City: Hustlers, Strivers, Dealers, Call Girls and Other Lives in Illicit New York*

Sendhil Mullainathan & Eldar Shafir, *Scarcity: Why Having Too Little Means So Much*

John Drury, *Music at Midnight: The Life and Poetry of George Herbert*

Philip Coggan, *The Last Vote: The Threats to Western Democracy*

Richard Barber, *Edward III and the Triumph of England*

Daniel M Davis, *The Compatibility Gene*

John Bradshaw, *Cat Sense: The Feline Enigma Revealed*

Roger Knight, *Britain Against Napoleon: The Organisation of Victory, 1793-1815*

Thurston Clarke, *JFK's Last Hundred Days: An Intimate Portrait of a Great President*

Jean Drèze and Amartya Sen, *An Uncertain Glory: India and its Contradictions*

Rana Mitter, *China's War with Japan, 1937-1945: The Struggle for Survival*

Tom Burns, *Our Necessary Shadow: The Nature and Meaning of Psychiatry*

Sylvain Tesson, *Consolations of the Forest: Alone in a Cabin in the Middle Taiga*

George Monbiot, *Feral: Searching for Enchantment on the Frontiers of Rewilding*

Ken Robinson and Lou Aronica, *Finding Your Element: How to Discover Your Talents and Passions and Transform Your Life*

David Stuckler and Sanjay Basu, *The Body Economic: Why Austerity Kills*

Suzanne Corkin, *Permanent Present Tense: The Man with No Memory, and What He Taught the World*

Daniel C. Dennett, *Intuition Pumps and Other Tools for Thinking*

Adrian Raine, *The Anatomy of Violence: The Biological Roots of Crime*

Eduardo Galeano, *Children of the Days: A Calendar of Human History*

Lee Smolin, *Time Reborn: From the Crisis of Physics to the Future of the Universe*

Michael Pollan, *Cooked: A Natural History of Transformation*

David Graeber, *The Democracy Project: A History, a Crisis, a Movement*

Brendan Simms, *Europe: The Struggle for Supremacy, 1453 to the Present*